ANNULORUM EXPERIMENTA

or

The Experiments of the Rings

Annulorum Experimenta

ISBN 978-1-915933-44-7 (HB)
ISBN 978-1-915933-45-4 (PB)
ISBN 978-1-915933-46-1 (Ebook)

A catalogue for this title is available from the British Library.
10 9 8 7 6 5 4 3 2 1

Published in 2024
Hadean Press
West Yorkshire
England

www.hadeanpress.com

ANNULORUM EXPERIMENTA

or

The Experiments of the Rings

by

Peter of Abano

Edited and Translated by

Regulus Hess

CONTENTS

INTRODUCTION

Peter of Abano stands together with Albertus Magnus, Roger Bacon, and Michael Scot among those towering figures of medieval learning who acquired in death a tremendous reputation for magic. Born around 1250 in a village near the city of Padua, he studied abroad for a long while in Constantinople and Paris, and perhaps elsewhere, before returning to his fatherland to teach at the university and practice medicine. Renowned for his erudition and medical skill, he attracted the fury of lesser minds and was accused of the heresy of materialism. Being, however, preserved from the flames by papal intervention, he was accused a second time in his old age, but departed this life before the trial was finished, thus escaping the hand of his persecutors forever.[1]

In examining his copious accepted writings, it must be noted for our purposes that they evince an unusual interest in the occult: not only in the natural magic and astrology condoned at the time by the shifting standards of Catholic moral theology, but even in those "necromantic" types of magic bordering on the forbidden. Thus in his greatest work, the *Conciliator*, we find this receipt for a talisman: "I have learned by experience that the figure of a lion impressed on gold while the Sun stands at the midheaven with Cor Leonis, Jupiter or Venus making an aspect thereto and the malefics being unfortunate and

1 For further reading on Peter of Abano in English, see Thorndike, pp. 874–947, and Barrett, pp. 155–157.

cadent, takes away the pain of the kidneys."[2] In another chapter he lists the names of the planetary "intelligences or angels", as follows: "The first is that of Saturn: Cassiel. The second, of Jupiter: Sachiel. The third, of Mars: Samael. The fourth, of the Sun: Michael. The fifth, of Venus: Anael. The sixth, of Mercury: Raphael. The seventh, of the Moon: Gabriel."[3] In the same work again, he tells of how "when the kings of the Greeks wished to make a petition to God concerning some business, they placed the Head of the Dragon at the midheaven with Jupiter, or aspected by the same with some amicable figure, the Moon being conjunct with Jupiter, or receding therefrom and applying to a conjunction with the lord of the ascendant, but still in an amicable figure with the Head", wherewith he concludes: "And it was said that their request would be heard."[4] Another talisman appears in *De venenis*, his celebrated treatise on poisons and their remedies, thus: "There is yet another thing, which is written in the *Book of the Persian Kings*, that if thou engravest upon hematite a man with bended knees who has a serpent girded about him, the head of which he holds in his right hand and the tail in his left: if thou placest this stone in a golden ring, putting under the stone the crushed root of adderwort, and bear this ring, it will preserve thee from every poison. Indeed, I have sometimes caused the same to be prepared, and to be

2 Diff. X, f. 17r, G.

3 Diff. IX, f. 15r, B.

4 Diff. CLVI, f. 213r, C, citing Sadan, *Excerpta de secretis Albumasar* 8, p. 303.

laid aside for the aforesaid use."[5] In a third work dealing with astrology he makes mention of several necromantic books he had been "going through", including the earliest known reference to the *Key of Solomon* in Latin, but describes them as "utterly obscene and depraved in understanding."[6]

Hence it will be seen that the accepted writings of Peter of Abano represent him as at least a dabbler in astrological magic, otherwise curious in his researches, but restrained by pious fear. Yet after his death there circulated rumors that he was much more than this, a magician of the first order in fact. The irony of this turn of events was not lost on some, such as Jean Bodin, who notes how Peter, as it had been alleged, endeavored to teach that there was no such thing as spirits, yet had been revealed to be "one of the greatest sorcerers of Italy."[7] For the legends say he was no mere dabbler, but a potent thaumaturge who kept seven familiar spirits enclosed in crystal, which furnished his prodigious knowledge of the liberal arts; and claim, moreover, that he had the power to move a well from one place to another, and to recall whatever money he spent from the merchant's strongbox back to his purse.[8] Three books of magic are traditionally ascribed to him. Two of these are the *Heptameron* and *Lucidarium*, whereof an edition and translation have

5 Cap. IV, pp. 23–24. The cited *Liber regum Persarum*, apparently no longer extant under that name, was a version of what has come down to us as *Liber Ptolomei de lapidibus preciosis et sigillis eorum* (for which, see the bibliography).

6 *Lucidator*, diff. I, p. 117.

7 *De la démonomanie des sorciers*, preface.

8 These tales are recounted briefly by Ferrari, p. 479.

recently been published:[9] third, quite different from those, is the *Annulorum experimenta*, which we intend to set forth in the present volume.

Now, while some modern scholars seem confident to style the writer of this book "Pseudo-" Peter of Abano, the question of his authorship remains a matter of doubt. As a magician at a time when the enemies of magic openly exercised power over life and death, it would have been necessary for the Peter of legend to keep his true vocation a secret, all the while dissimulating about his religious and philosophical convictions, and not to allow a spell-book bearing his name to circulate till after his decease. One thing curious to note is the resemblance between the tales of Peter's exploits and the operations we find herein. Would you have a familiar spirit to teach you the liberal arts? Read chapter thirty-one. Would you discover the secret of the miraculous well? Read chapter twenty-five. Would you spend the same money again and again? Read chapter twenty-eight. One almost gets the impression that Peter's legend is based on the *Experimenta*.

The earliest extant writer to mention this work is Abbot Trithemius. Himself a reputed magician whom we cannot help suspecting of his own theological dissimulation, he refers to our author as "Peter of Abano, the Paduan physician, called the Conciliator, of whom many fabulous things are told", and lists the *Experimenta* under "books having no manifest communion with daemons", yet "greatly to be feared" by reason of their methods: calling it *Liber experimentorum de annulis mirabilium*

9 See *Elucidation of Necromancy*, edited and translated by Joseph H. Peterson.

secundum 28 mansiones lunae. This reference appears in his well-known "Bibliography for Necromancers",[10] written in 1508, nearly 200 years after Peter's death in 1316. Meanwhile, the oldest manuscript of the *Experimenta* is of Italian provenance, dating back to the fifteenth century, but evidently a copy of one produced in the latter part of the 1300s.[11] The late fourteenth century has thus been surmised as the period of the text's composition, but we see no reason why it might not be older, apart from the pedantic bias against Peter's own authorship.

The book consists of two parts. First is a listing of the mansions of the Moon, the twenty-eight celestial stations through which the luminary is said to pass over the course of its monthly circuit. These seem to derive from the astronomy of the ancient Indians, passed down to the Latins through Arabic writings such as the *Picatrix*, which latter employs them in its own magical operations.[12] The second and principal part of the text consists of forty "experiments" based on the positions of the Moon in these mansions. It lays down a method combining this kind of astrological timing with prayers to the supreme deity and the conjuration of spirits, along with magical characters, suffumigations, and so forth, for the construction and use

10 Text in Zambelli, pp. 101–112.

11 See Boudet, pp. 251–252.

12 It should be noted here that Peter's posthumous detractors accused him of borrowing from this very book. The ill-fated obscurantist Giovanni Francesco Pico della Mirandola (nephew of the famous Pico) avers for example: "I suspect Aponensis drew a great part of these things from the *Picatrix*, a book most vain, full of superstitions and erected as a ladder to idolatry" (*De praenotione rerum*, lib. 7, cap. 7).

of magical rings and the performance of various magical feats. Thus we seem to find elements herein of both the Hermetic magic of the *Picatrix* and the Solomonic magic of the *Heptameron*.

THE MANUSCRIPTS

P Paris, Bibliothèque Nationale de France, Lat. 7337, 15th cen., pp. 131–138.

A Augsburg, Universitätsbibliothek, Cod. II.I.4, 15th cen., ff. 19r–20r.

G Ghent, Universiteitsbibliotheek, 1021A, 16th cen., ff. 98r–107r.

L London, Society of Antiquaries, MS 39, 15th cen., ff. 2r–6v.

Lü Lübeck, Stadtbibliothek, MS Math. 4° 9, 16th cen., ff. 150v–152v.

O Oxford, Bodleian Library, Rawlinson MS D.252, 15th cen., ff. 96r–97r.

THE EDITION AND TRANSLATION

The *Annulorum experimenta* survives, to our knowledge, in six copies. First is that of P, the Paris manuscript, not only the oldest, but also the sole complete and unabridged specimen of the text. Second is that of A, the Augsburg manuscript, which closely follows the readings in P, but unfortunately stops after just a few chapters. Third is that of G, the Ghent manuscript, more corrupt than A, and missing large portions of the text. Fourth is that of L, the London manuscript, a shortened reworking largely focused on the chapters with magical characters. Fifth is that of Lü, the Lübeck manuscript, which carries a general abridgment of the text. Sixth is that of O, the Oxford manuscript, containing a few selected chapters.

Given this state of affairs, our task as editor has been greatly simplified. We began with a transcription from P to establish a base-text. Following this, we have used the other manuscripts to correct the errors P contains, and supply the omissions. All readings, as well as the characters, are according to P unless otherwise stated. Obvious mistakes, such as mechanical repetitions, have been emended silently. Alternative readings of interest have been added in the footnotes, particularly those of the names of the spirits, which are given according to all the manuscripts wherever we have found them.

Together with this new edition,[13] we provide the first published English translation of the *Annulorum experimenta*—written, we hope, in the solemn and literal style which seems to the translator most befitting the literature of medieval magic.

NOTE ON THE APPENDICES

Following the conclusion of this work, the reader will find three appendices. The first gives the forms of the magical characters as they appear throughout all the manuscripts. The second contains a translation of the *Anelli di Pietro d'Abano*, a unique vernacular tract related to the Latin

13 Note the previous edition of Boudet, pp. 270–286.

Experimenta. The third includes some extracts from the *Picatrix* chiefly concerning the nuances of astrological timing, a matter which should be undervalued neither by the scholar nor the aspiring magician.

EDITION

Petri de Abano Annulorum experimenta[14]

Peritissimi artium ac medicine doctoris in omnibusque scientiis excellentissimi magistri Petri de Abano[15] Annulorum experimenta feliciter incipiunt.

Primo et principaliter in hac arte considerandum est quod viginti octo sunt mansiones Lune, quarum quilibet dantur duodecim gradus zodyaci et minuta duodecim et secunde due.

Prima mansio Lune est caput Arietis.
Secunda est venter Arietis.
Tertia est finis Arietis.
Quarta est caput Tauri et venter.
Quinta est finis Tauri et Geminorum principium.
Sexta est venter Geminorum.
Septima est finis Geminorum.
Octava est caput Cancri.
Nona est venter Cancri.
Decima est finis Cancri et caput Leonis.
Undecima est venter Leonis.
Duodecima est finis Leonis et principium Virginis.
Tertiadecima est venter Virginis.

---

14 Petri . . . experimenta. *P* / Petri de Apono Experimenta *A* / De annulorum fabricatione sub mantionibus Lune clarrisimi viri Petri de Abano qui et compliator dicitur liber *G* / Experimenta annulorum peritissimi Petri de Abano *Lü*

15 Abano *editor* / Abbano *PA*

Quartadecima est finis Virginis.
Quintadecima est caput Libre.
Sextadecima est venter Libre.
Septimadecima est finis Libre et principium Scorpionis.
Octavadecima est venter Scorpionis.
Nonadecima est finis Scorpionis et caput Sagittarii.
Vicesima est venter Sagittarii.
Vicesima prima est finis Sagittarii.
Vicesima secunda est caput Capricorni.
Vicesima tertia est venter Capricorni
Vicesima quarta est finis Capricorni et caput Aquarii.[16]
Vicesima quinta est venter Aquarii.
Vicesima sexta est finis Aquarii et caput Piscium.
Vicesima septima est venter Piscium.
Vicesima octava et ultima est finis Piscium.

Expliciunt mansiones Lune.

Et nota quod prima mansio Lune dicitur esse illa per quam currit per diem et noctem Luna; et secunda et tertia, et sic de aliis similiter currunt.

16 Vicesima tertia . . . caput Aquarii. *editor* / 23. Venter Capricorni. 24. Finis Capricorni et caput Aquarii. *ALü* / 22 est caput Capricorni. 23 est venter Capricorni et caput Aquarii. *P*

I. Ut appareat flumen in aere

Prima[17] mansione Lune, fac fieri annulum argenteum, in cujus concavitate ponantur ista nomina[18] scripta in pergameno virgineo:

Pharai.[19] Murath.[20] Lamerthe.[21] Baroy.[22]

Et sint ista nomina scripta cum sanguine anguille, et sit annulus sine lapide. Annulo completo sine foramine, teneas ipsum die sequenti in aurora diei super ripam alicujus fluminis; et habeas os apertum versus flumen flexis genibus, dicendo hanc orationem sequentem. Et suffumiga annulum cum thure.

Oratio: "Domine Deus omnipotens, qui de celo summo vides abissum, per quem vivunt viventes et moriuntur morientes, qui populum Pharaonis[23] in aquis marinis submersisti, et qui in deserto fontem erexisti: largitatem tue benignitatis exoro, quatenus quacumque die vel hora tetigero istum annulum cum saliva mea, isti quattuor spiritus quorum nomina sunt hic intus[24] inclusa faciant unum mirabile flumen quandocumque voluero et ubicumque absque mora viriliter apparere."

---

17 Prima *PAG* / In prima *L*

18 nomina *PAG* / 4or nomina angelorum *L*

19 Pharai *PAG* / Pharay *L* / Phoray *Lü*

20 Murath *P* / Anrath *A* / Mirath *GLü* / Gudrai *L*

21 Lamerthe *A* / Lumen *G* / Lunere *L* / Lamerthei *Lü* / *P om.*

22 Baroy *P* / Baray *AGLü* / Berai *L*

23 Pharaonis *AG* / Pharonis *P*

24 intus *G* / *PA om.*

Hoc facto, tangas aquam cum annulo, faciendo hoc signum:

Hoc facto, involvas dictum annulum in sindone albo et custodi mundissime. Et cum volueris operari, tange annulum cum saliva,[25] sic dicendo:

"O vos spiritus, quorum nomina sunt inclusa in hoc annulo, conjuro atque adjuro vos, per illum cui debetis principaliter obedire, et per hanc sacratissimam orationem supradictam, et per omnia sanctissima nomina Dei, et per omnes sanctos et sanctas Dei celestis curie, quatenus sub pena eternalis ignis, sine mora pulcrum flumen vel lacum vel mare quod desidero in tali loco apperere faciatis."

II. AD IDEM FACIENDUM

Fac fieri annulum prima mansione Lune et sicut superius fecisti; sed annulus sit ferreus concavus, in cujus concavitate ponantur ista nomina in pergameno communi:

STORPHALUS. PARPALIN. GUROHRIT.[26]

---

25 cum saliva *AG* / cum sindone saliva *P*

26 Storphalus. . . . Gurohrit. *P* / Storphalus. . . . Gurohrith. *A* / Strophalus. Parpolin. Gurorhrith. *G* / Scrophalo. Parpalin. Gurolarith. *Lü*

Annulo completo, suffumiga ipsum cum viscu querci et sanguine arietis, dicendo, "Domine Deus omnipotens, etc.", ut supra dixisti. Hoc facto, tange flumen cum annulo. Et cum volueris operari, dicas ut supra, etc.

III. Ut cervus et canes inter se sequentes appareant

Secunda mansione Lune, fac fieri annulum argenteum concavum, in cujus concavitate ponantur ista nomina scripta in pergameno virgineo cum sanguine cervi et canis in simul mixto:

Anna. Heasil. Sorphail. Vacerail.[27]

Annulo completo et foramine obtuso, teneas ipsum in aurora diei sequentis in introitu alicujus nemoris, et suffumiga cum mirra et aloe. Et habeas os[28] apertum versus nemus, et flexis genibus hanc dicas orationem.

Oratio:[29] "Domine Deus omnipotens, qui de celo summo vides abissum, per quem vivunt viventes et moriuntur morientes, qui silvas magnas et alia nascentia in mundo fecisti: largitatem tue benignitatis exoro, quatenus quacumque die vel hora ego tangam annulum cum saliva mea, illi spiritus quorum nomina sunt in hoc annulo inclusa faciant cervum et duos canes sequentes

---

27 Anna. . . . Vacerail. *PA* / Anna. Teasil. Sorozayl. Vaterayl. *G* / Annā. Veasid. Corsayl. Varoayl. *L* / Amathealilis. Sorphail. Vaterail. *Lü*

28 os *AG* / *P om.*

29 Oratio *A* / *PG om.*

ante oculos meos[30] vel cujuscumque voluero sine mora pervenire."

Hoc dicto, tangas terram cum annulo, faciendo hoc signum:

Hoc paratum, involvas annulum in syndone viridi et custodi mundissime. Et cum volueris tangere annulum cum saliva, dicas sic:

"O vos spiritus, quorum nomina sunt in hoc annulo inclusa, conjuro atque adjuro vos per illum cui tenemini principaliter obedire, quatenus incontinenti quod desidero viriliter faciatis."

Hoc facto, videbis cervum et canes et alia mirabilia.

IV. UT CARCERATUS POSSET DE CARCERE ET CATHENIS LIBERARI

Secunda mansione Lune, fac fieri annulum ferreum concavum, in cujus concavitate ponantur hec nomina scripta in pergameno virgineo, scilicet:

QUADRA. BRIMETH.[31]

Annulo completo, perge in introitu alicujus turris; et suffumiga dictum annulum cum capillis latronum,

30 meos *AG* / *P om.*

31 Quadra. Brimeth. *P* / Quadribrimeth. *G* / Quadrabrimech. *Lü*

dicendo, "Domine Deus, etc." Postea tange cathenas cum dicto annulo, et sine dubio videbis carceratum liberari.

V. UT MILITES ARMATI APPAREANT

Tertia mansione Lune, fac fieri annulum aureum concavum, in cujus concavitate ponantur ista nomina scripta in pergameno virgineo de sanguine alicujus hominis, scilicet:

ANELIM. ALIBEAT. ESTADE. BOAD. BARTIFARI.[32]

Annulo completo, teneas ipsum sequenti die in aurora diei in introitu alicujus campi, et suffumiga cum dentibus alicujus hominis mortui; et dicas versus campum hanc sequentem orationem.

Oratio:[33] "Domine Deus omnipotens, qui de celo summo[34] ultimos vides abissos, qui hominem ad ymaginem et similitudinem tuam formasti, per quem vivunt viventes et moriuntur morientes: largitatem tue benignitatis exoro, quatenus quacumque die vel hora tangam annulum istum cum saliva mea, isti spiritus quorum nomina sunt hic intus inclusa faciant armatos milites bellantes ante oculos meos vel cujuscumque voluero apparere[35] viriliter."

---

32 Anelim. . . . Bartifari *P* / Anelin. *(?)* Alibeat. Estad. Bartifari. *G* / Danebta. Alibiat. Stablocth. Virciseri. *L* / Anelim. Alibrat. Esead. Baad. Bartifaci. *Lü*

33 Oratio *editor* / *PG om.*

34 summo *G* / *P om.*

35 apparere *G* / *P om.*

Hoc dicto, tange terram cum annulo, faciendo hoc signum:

Postea annulum involve in syndone nigro, et mundissime custodias. Et cum volueris operari, dicas tangendo annulum cum saliva:

"O vos spiritus, quorum nomina sunt hic intus inclusa, conjuro vos atque adjuro per illum cui tenemini obedire, quatenus quacumque desidero incontinenti faciatis."

Hoc facto, videbis milites bellantes sine dubio.

VI. Ut in una hora centum miliaria possis ambulare sine lesione

Tertia mansione Lune, fac fieri annulum aureum concavum, in cujus concavitate ponantur hec nomina scripta in pergameno virgineo, scilicet:

FARIMAN. BERGATH. BUTHATH.[36]

Annulo completo, vadas in aurora diei sequentis in introitu alicujus nemoris; et suffumiga dictum annulum cum viscu querci et stercore equino, dicendo, "O Domine Deus, etc.", quatenus "michi appareat spiritus cujus nomen in hoc annulo clausum est in forma equi, qui me deferat secure sine aliqua lesione corporis et anime." Sed nec retro aspicias, nec te signes, cum super equum fueris.

36 Fariman. . . . Buthath. *P* / Farinam. Bengath. Buthath. *G* / Farinam. Bengath. Bntach. *Lü*

VII. UT PERGULA CUM RAMIS ET VINIS FERTILIBUS APPAREAT

Quarta mansione Lune, fac fieri annulum aureum concavum, in cujus concavitate ponantur ista nomina scripta in pergameno virgineo, scilicet, cum incausto[37] spinarum:

HERADI. HATIARIE. FASTUR. CRAULYARUY.[38]

Annulo completo, teneas ipsum die sequenti in aurora diei in introitu alicujus vinee, dicendo hec verba versus vineas:

"Domine Deus qui olim aquam in vinum mutasti, qui de ultimo celo vides abissum, per quem vivunt viventes et moriuntur morientes: largitatem tue benignitatis exoro, quatenus quacumque die vel hora tangam annulum istum cum saliva mea, spiritus illi quorum nomina sunt hic intus inclusa ornatam vineam cum racemis apparere faciant sine aliqua mora ante oculos meos ubicumque voluero."

Hoc facto, tange terram cum annulo, faciendo hoc signum:

37 cum incausto *L* / *P om.*

38 Heradi. . . . Craulyaruy *P* / Berhadi. Hacatusasturer. Itanlid. Ruy. *L* / Spinarium vel spiratum. Scilum. Heradi. Batriatie. Fastur. Craulis. Nuis. *Lü*

Hoc facto, involve eum in sindone viridi[39] et custodi mundissime. Et cum volueris operari, fac ut in aliis supradictis.

VIII. De duobus bellantibus vel litigantibus facias quem vis superare

Quarta mansione, fac fieri annulum ferreum concavum, in cujus concavitate ponantur ista nomina scripta in pergameno communi, scilicet:

FAMUAR. CHULYARIB.[40]

Die sequenti, teneas dictum annulum in camera tua; et fumiga ipsum cum viscu querci et cum cera virginea, dicendo, "Domine Deus, etc.",[41] ut supra: nec aliquid de misse de vinea, sed dicas, "Cuicumque hunc annulum dedero sive tradidero tua sit virtute contra suum hostem; sive triumphans existat."[42] Hoc facto, custodi dictum annulum mundissime in sindone albissimo. Et cum volueris operari, fac ut supra in aliis fecisti.

IX. Ut nemora cum silvis et pratis viridibus appareant

Quinta mansione Lune, fac fieri annulum cupreum concavum, in cujus concavitate ponantur ista nomina

---

39 eum in sindone viridi *L* / in sindone annulum *P*

40 Famuar. Chulyarib. *P* / Famiar. Chichy. Cirih. *Lü*

41 etc. *editor* / *P om.*

42 existat *Lü* / *P om.*

scripta in pergameno virgineo cum sanguine lacerti viridis, scilicet:

Osturies. Bragandi. Jucamischada. Pachimisca.[43]

Annulo completo, teneas ipsum die sequenti in aurora in introitu alicujus prati; et suffumiga annulum cum feno. Sed capite inclinato versus pratum dicas sic:

"O Domine Deus omnipotens, qui de celo ultimo vides abyssum, qui diversas herbas crescere promisisti, per quem vivunt viventes et moriuntur morientes: largitatem tue benignitatis exoro, quatenus quacumque die vel hora tangam istum annulum cum saliva mea, spiritus illi quorum nomina sunt hic intus inclusa nemora pulcra cum floribus et viridibus pratis apparere faciant sine mora aliqua ante nostros oculos quandocumque[44] et ubicumque voluero."

Hoc dicto, tange cum annulo terram, faciendo hoc signum:

Postea involve annulum in panno lini non operato, et mundissime custodi. Et cum volueris operari, fac ut dictum est.

---

43 Osturies. . . . Pachimisca. *P* / Asuraes. Bitradandibi. Hannistada. Pathinisiti. *L* / Astaries. Bragandi. Vitamiscada. Pachimisra. *Lü*

44 quandocumque *editor* / quocumque *P*

X. UT INIMICUS TUUS QUACUMQUE VIS INFIRMITATE INFIRMETUR

Quinta mansione, fac fieri annulum plumbeum, in cujus concavitate ponatur istud nomen scriptum[45] in pergameno communi, scilicet:

HABRACULITH.[46]

Die sequenti, teneas ipsum annulum in aliquo trivio; et flexis genibus, suffumiga ipsum cum stercore humano, dicendo, "Domine Deus, etc." Sed muta petitionem sic, dicendo ut "quecumque tangam vel tangere faciam cum annulo isto talis egrotet infirmitate, etc." Postea cum volueris operari, tange annulum cum saliva; et mundissime custodi in sindone nigro, etc.

XI. UT MENSA FERTILIBUS ORNATA VARIISQUE PANNIS CIBISQUE VIDEATUR

Sexta mansione Lune, fac fieri annulum concavum stagneum, in cujus concavitate ponantur ista nomina scripta in pergameno virgineo cum sanguine bovis, scilicet:

BARDARI. ACER. PREDO. GAMMAGANDARVI. HASTAPULO.[47]

---

45 istud . . . scriptum *P* / haec nomina scripta *Lü*

46 Habraculith. *P* / Habaratuch. Habaratulis. *Lü*

47 Bardari. . . . Hastapulo. *P* / Badari. Acer. Perdo. Gammagandarvi. Astanulo. *G* / Adariantur. Perdogamma. Cauda. Rupasta. *L* / Sardart. Acorperdo. Santryagamdor. *Lü*

Annulo completo, etc., teneas ipsum in aurora diei sequentis in introitu alicujus coquine; et suffumiga ipsum cum cerebro porci, et inclinato capite dicas versus coquinam:

"Domine Deus omnipotens, etc., erga quem non sunt aliqua abscondita, per quem vivunt viventes et moriuntur morientes: largitatem tue benignitatis exoro, quatenus quacumque die vel hora tangam annulum istum cum saliva mea, spiritus illi quorum nomina sunt hic intus posita mensam pulcram et fertilem ornatam diversis cibis apparere ante oculos nostros faciant sine aliqua mora quandocumque et ubicumque[48] voluero."

Hoc dicto, tange terram cum annulo, faciendo hoc signum:

Hoc facto, involve annulum in panno lineo et custodi mundissime. Et cum operari volueris, fac ut dictum est prius cum modis et rebus requisitis.

XII. Ut infirmus gaudium recuperat et sanetur

Sexta mansione Lune, fac fieri annulum aureum concavum, in cujus concavitate ponantur ista nomina scripta in pergameno virgineo, scilicet:

48 ubicumque *editor* / uicumque *P* / *G om.*

DARATEES. ESORUM. TINCHIR.[49]

Annulo completo, etc., suffumiga ipsum in aliqua camera[50] cum thure et cera virginea, dicendo, "Domine Deus, etc.", ut supra nunc scriptum est, ut "quemcumque vel quacumque tangam vel tangere cum annulo isto[51] faciam gaudium recuperet et tali liberetur[52] infirmitate, etc." Hoc facto, custodi dictum annulum mundissime in syndone azuro. Et cum volueris operari fac ut supra.

XIII. UT ARBOR APPAREAT CUM FRUCTU VEL SINE FRUCTU UT VIS

In septima mansione, fac fieri annulum ferreum concavum, in cujus concavitate ponantur hec nomina scripta in pergameno virgineo, scilicet:

CAMBRISTAY. ANURECHA. FARASTARIO.[53]

Annulo completo, etc., teneas ipsum in aurora diei sequentis in introitu alicujus viridarii;[54] et capite inclinato dictum annulum suffumiga cum ligno aloes, dicendo, "Domine Deus, etc.", faciendo petitionem quam vis

49 Daratees . . . Tinchir. *P* / Daratees. Estorum. Tinchir. *G* / Dairates. Esorum. Tinchir. *Lü*

50 in aliqua camera *PG* / in camera tua *Lü*

51 cum annulo isto *Lü* / *P om.*

52 liberetur *GLü* / libentur *P*

53 Cambristay. . . . Farastario. *P* / Cambristay. Ammurach. Farastario. *G* / Camhe. Ystoy. Amaretha. Sastarie. *L* / Cambistray. Amirech. Facascacio. *Lü*

54 viridarii *GL* / jardini *P*

sicut in aliis fecisti. Hoc facto, tange terram, faciendo hos caracteres:

Postea volve dictum annulum in syndone croceo. Et cum volueris operari, fac ut in aliis, etc.

XIV. UT COMMEDENTES VERMES RACEMOS COMMEDERE VIDEANTUR

Septima mansione, fac fieri annulum stagneum concavum, in cujus concavitate ponantur ista nomina scripta in pergameno communi, scilicet:

HYERSERUS. MAURNATH. NAURSTIC.[55]

Annulo completo, teneas ipsum die sequenti in aurora in camera tua; et ipsum suffumiga cum vermiculis terrestribus, dicendo, "Domine Deus, etc.", sed mutando petitionem, ut "quicumque tenebit hunc annulum et vermes ei ante ponantur virtute istorum spirituum hic intus inclusorum racemos vinearum commedere videatur[56] quandocumque et ubicumque voluero."[57]

---

55 Hyerserus. . . . Naurstic. *P* / Hiererserus. Muirnath. Muirstich. *G*

56 videatur *editor per cap. XVI* / videantur *PG*

57 voluero *G* / volueris *P*

XV. UT QUERCUS DIVERSIS AVIBUS ET FLORIBUS APPARERE VIDEATUR

Octava mansione Lune, fac fieri annulum de radice quercus, in quo sit scriptum hoc nomen:

RARIATH.[58]

Annulo completo, teneas[59] ipsum in introitu alicujus nemoris quercuum; et suffumiga de foliis quercus, capite inclinato, dicendo, "Domine Deus, etc.", ut "quandocumque voluero spiritus ille cujus nomen est intus inclusum sine mora faciat pulcram quercum diversis avibus et foliis decoratam ante nostros oculos vel ubicumque voluero penitus apparere, etc." Hoc facto, tange terram cum annulo, faciendo hoc signum:

Et involve in bombace.[60] Et cum operari volueris, fac ut prius, tangens[61] annulum cum saliva tua; et fac omnia requisita ut in aliis fecisti, etc.

---

58 Rariath. *PLü* / Barath. *G* / Beroth. *L*

59 teneas *editor* / suffumiga *P*

60 Et involve in bombace. *L* / *PG om.*

61 fac ut prius, tangens *G* / fac ut tangas *P*

XVI. Ut commedentes racemos vermes commedere videantur

Octava mansione, fac fieri annulum argenteum concavum, in cujus concavitate ponatur istud nomen scriptum in carta virginea,[62] scilicet:

Saufaole.[63]

In die sequenti, etc., in aurora diei, suffumiga ipsum in aliquo campo cum uva, dicendo, "Domine Deus, etc.", sed mutando petitionem ut dicendo, "Quicumque tenebit hunc annulum et racemi ei ante ponantur virtute hujus spiritus hic inclusi vermes terrestres commedere videatur quandocumque et ubicumque voluero." Et cum operari volueris, facias ut in aliis, etc.

XVII. Ut mus videatur post se trahere molam molendini

Nona mansione, fac fieri annulum argenteum concavum, in cujus concavitate ponantur hec nomina in pergameno virgineo scripta, scilicet:

Trellari. Yenuat. Bournes. Bournay. Syeth.[64]

---

62 carta virginea *P* / pergameno virgineo *G*

63 Saniferole. *(?) G*

64 Trellari. . . . Syeth. *P* / Trelariyeunat. Bournes. Vournay. Syeth. *G* / Treleatye. Ymas. Bournos. Beurnxioth. *L* / Trelare. Yennat. Bournes. Bournay. Syeth. *Lü*

Annulo completo, etc., in aurora diei sequentis, vade in introitu alicujus molendini; et suffumiga ipsum cum blado, dicendo, "Domine Deus, etc.", sed mutando petitionem, ut "spiritus illi quorum nomina sunt hic intus inclusa eorum virtute faciant ante nostros oculos apparere murem molam molendini post se trahantem, sub pena eternalis ignis, etc."

Hoc facto, tange terram cum annulo prope aquam limitis molendini faciendo hoc signum:

Hoc facto, involve dictum annulum in corio muris et mundissime custodi. Et cum operari volueris, fac ut in aliis, etc.

XVIII. Ut homo qualiscumque sit dimittat domum suam et fugiat

Nona mansione, fac fieri annulum plumbeum concavum, in cujus concavitate ponantur ista nomina scripta in pergameno virgineo, scilicet:

JEARTAAG. BELLICORTH. SIRGITH.[65]

Die autem sequenti, suffumiga cum sulfure in latrina, dicendo ter nomina predicta. Postea tange cum annulo

65 Jeartaag. . . . Sirgith. *P* / Carcaag. Bellicaert. Sirgith. *G* / Cartaas. Bellicort. Sirgit. *Lü*

terram,[66] etc. Et cum operari volueris, fac ut supra in aliis, etc.

XIX. Ut lectus cum culcitis, lintheaminibus et aliis pulcris ornamentis appareat

Decima mansione Lune, fac fieri annulum aureum concavum, in cujus concavitate ponantur hec nomina scripta in pergameno communi, scilicet:

Bernerecha. Baxo. Monego. Difinicha.[67]

Annulo completo, vade in aurora diei sequentis in introitu alicujus camere, et suffumiga dictum annulum cum pannis novis, dicendo inclinato capite, "Domine Deus,[68] etc.", sicut "illi spiritus quorum nomina sunt in hoc annulo inclusa sua virtute faciant ante oculos nostros et cujuscumque voluero pulcrum lectum ornamentis omnibus ornatum viriliter apparere, sub pena eternalis ignis, etc."

Hoc facto, tange terram cum annulo, faciendo istud signum:

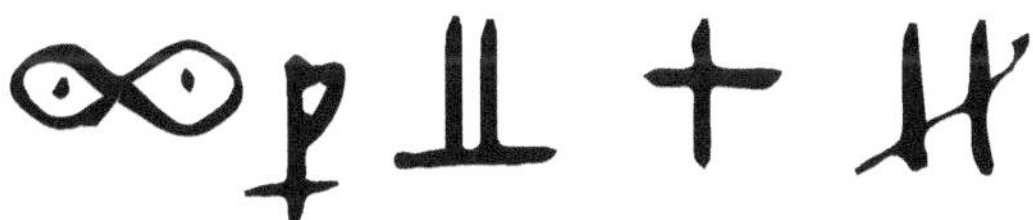

66 tange cum annulo terram *editor* / tange annulo terram *Lü* / annulum cum terra *P*

67 Bernerecha. . . . Difinicha. *P* / Bernerecha. Bajo. Anego. Diffiton. *G* / Bernerech. Bayd. Monego. Disamata. *L* / Burnerechia. Bayomonego. Diffnniha. *Lü*

68 Domine Deus *G* / Deus, Deus *P*

Postea involve in aliquo frusto alicujus panni lini novi operati. Et cum operari volueris, fac ut supra.

XX. Ut thesaurum absconditum possis subtiliter invenire

Decima mansione, fac fieri annulum aureum concavum, in cujus concavitate ponatur hoc nomen scriptum in pergameno virgineo, scilicet:

Heusenebior.[69]

Die sequenti, suffumiga ipsum in aurora, in camera tua cum feniculo et thure, dicendo, "Domine Deus, etc." Et dormiendo, pone dictum annulum sub capite tuo et videbis in sompnio ubi est thesaurus. Et custodi mundissime in syndone turchino; et cum operari volueris, dic et fac ut in aliis.

XXI. Ut elefas portans castrum viriliter appareat

Undecima mansione, fac fieri annulum eburneum non concavum sed in costis scriptum hoc nomen, scilicet:

Fernagitim.[70]

Annulo completo, vade in aurora diei sequentis in introitu alicujus castri; et suffumiga dictum annulum cum

69 Heusenebior. *P* / Herusenebior. *G* / Heusebrocor. *O*

70 Fernagitim. *P* / Farnagircim. *G* / Formagatom *L* / Fernagirthim. *Lü*

ebore et capillis hominum vivorum, dicendo, "Domine Deus, etc.", sed mutando petitionem. sicut "spiritus ille cujus nomen est in hoc annulo insignitum sua virtute faciat mirabilem elefantem apparere castrum portantem, etc." Hoc facto, tange terram cum annulo, faciendo hoc signum:

Hoc facto, custodi dictum annulum mundissime in pixide eburneo.[71] Et cum operari volueris, fac ut in aliis.

XXII. UT DOMUS VEL VILLA VISIBILITER ARDERE VIDEATUR[72]

Undecima mansione, fac fieri annulum aureum concavum, in cujus concavitate ponantur hec nomina scripta in pergameno virgineo, scilicet:

GARIDOLICALU. FURINICAT. BRACHUCAL.[73]

Die sequenti in aurora diei, suffumiga ipsum in introitu alicujus ville vel domus, dicendo, "Domine Deus, etc.", ut "quacumque[74] domum vel villam cum isto annulo circumiverit, illi spiritus quorum nomina sunt hic

---

71 in pixide eburneo *L* / *PG om.*

72 Ut . . . videatur *G* / *P om.*

73 Garidolicalu. . . . Brachucal. *P* / Gardosicolu. Furmicat. Baenschlal. *G* / Sardoich. Furineat. Banechichal. *Lü*

74 quacumque *G* / quicumque *P*

inclusa sua virtute videntibus faciant apparere domum sive villam viriliter ardere." Et hoc facto, annulum custodi mundissime in quocumque loco mundo.

XXIII. UT DRACO HORRIBILIS ET MAGNUS APPAREAT

Duodecima mansione, fac fieri annulum cupreum concavum, in cujus concavitate ponantur ista nomina scripta in pergameno communi,[75] scilicet:

DOMINATH. BORIATIACALI. ENAPRIA. TERIATH.[76]

Annulo completo, vade in aurora die sequentis in introitu alicujus prati, et suffumiga cum sanguine draconis, dicendo, "Domine Deus, etc." Hoc facto, tange terram cum[77] annulo, faciendo hoc signum:

Postea custodi in panno albo lineo non operato. Et cum operari volueris, fac ut supra.

---

75 communi *GL* / *P om.*

76 Dominath. . . . Teriath. *P* / Dominath. Borillatiacath. Enapria. Teriat. *G* / Derminte. Bartilanatab. Empro. Ateryeth. *L* / Dominath. Borilla. Tracali. Enapria. Tonath. *Lü*

77 cum *G* / *P om.*

XXIV. Ut quecumque vis facias deponere vestes suas

Duodecima mansione, fac fieri annulum stagneum concavum, in cujus concavitate ponatur hoc nomen scriptum in pergameno virgineo, scilicet:

Dordrachuth.[78]

Die sequenti in aurora, suffumiga ipsum in platea communi cum sanguine yrci, dicendo, "Domine Deus, etc.", ut "quicumque, etc."[79] Et fac[80] ut in aliis.

XXV. Ut fons vel puteus in campo vel in camera appareat

Tertiadecima mansione Lune, fac fieri annulum stagneum concavum, in cujus concavitate[81] sint scripta ista nomina,[82] scilicet:

Roder.[83] Pacorp.[84]

---

78 Dordrachuth *PLü* / Dordachut *G*

79 ut "quicumque etc." *P* / quatenus "quocumque *(sic)* die vel hora tetigero annulo isto *(sic)*, aliquis exuat vestes suas." *Lü*

80 Et fac *Lü* / *P om.*

81 concavum . . . concavitate *PG* / non concavum in quo *L*

82 scripta ista nomina *PG* / hec nomina scripta in pergameno communi *Lü*

83 Roder. *P* / Veder. *G* / Bober. *L* / Roderi. *Lü*

84 Pacorp. *G* / Pacoris. *(?) P* / Pelcorp. *L* / Pereaop. *Lü*

Annulo completo, in aurora sequentis diei, vade ad orificium cujusdam fontis vel putei et ibi suffumiga annullum cum aqua,[85] dicendo, "Domine Deus, etc." Hoc facto, tange aliquem lapidem orificii, faciendo hoc signum:

Hoc facto, custodi ipsum in fiala plena aqua clara. Et cum volueris operari, fac ut supra.

XXVI. UT CASTRUM CUM PERTINENTIBUS IN QUOCUMQUE LOCO VIS APPAREAT

Quartadecima mansione, fac fieri annulum[86] concavum, in cujus concavitate ponantur ista nomina scripta in pergameno virgineo, scilicet:

GORALIDIO. BRANDAMIROTH. SCAURIOCI.[87]

Annulo completo, in aurora diei sequentis, vade in introitu alicujus castri; et suffumiga dictum annulum cum calce viva, dicendo, "Domine Deus, etc."[88] Hoc facto, tange terram cum annulo, faciendo hoc signum:

---

85 aqua *GLü* / aquatica *P* / aqua calida *L*

86 annulum *PG* / annulum cupreum *L* / annulus argenteus *Lü*

87 Goralidio. . . . Scaurioci. *P* / Boralidio. Branda. Miroth. Samirioci. *G* / Gzigotalibet. Beaudaminet. Tunirioh. *L* / Goralidis. Brandamiroth. Scanrioth. *Lü*

88 etc. *G* / *P om.*

Postea involve ipsum in panno lineo nigro, etc.[89] Et cum operari volueris, fac ut supra.[90]

XXVII. Ut mons currens[91] domum sequi videatur

Quintadecima mansione, fac fieri pulverem de sanguine draconis et aloes et visci querci.[92] Et defer ipsum pulverem in aurora sequentis diei prope aliquem montem; et suffumiga ipsum cum terra ejusdem vel alterius montis, dicendo ista nomina:

Tertin. Moda. Brasilir. Godrir. Bodre.[93]

Et postea dic, "Domine Deus, etc." Quo facto custodi dictum pulverem in pixide argenti. Et cum operari volueris, sparge pulverem, ut ante.

---

89 Postea . . . etc. *L* / Serva mundissime. *Lü* / *PG om.*

90 Et cum . . . ut supra. *editor* / Et operari volueris fac ut supra. *G* / *P om.*

91 currens *P* / aureus *GLü*

92 visci querci *G* / visci quercini *P* / visco quercino *L*

93 Tertin. . . . Bodre. *P* / Terin. Modebrasilir. Bodre. *G* / Brafilis. Ghodiat. Bodith. *L* / Tartin. Moda. Brasilit. Banbrit. Bodre. *Lü*

XXVIII. Ut denarii quos expendisti ad te revertantur

Sextadecima mansione Lune, accipe denarios qualescumque vis et liga illos in syndone croceo et novo. Et suffumiga totum hoc cum viscu querci, dicendo:

"Domine Deus omnipotens, qui de ultimo celo vides abissos, qui homines ad ymaginem et similitudinem tuam formasti, per quem vivunt viventes et moriuntur morientes: largitatem tue benignitatis exoro, quatenus in quacumque die vel hora tangam sindone croceo cum saliva mea, isti videlicet spiritus quorum sunt intus inclusa faciant denarios ad me cum sociis suis revertantur in quacumque die vel hora."[94]

Et cum volueris expendere, dicas secretissime hec nomina:

GUBRIDALI. HARMUROCH. FRATRADRITH. GORMI.[95]

Et postea dic,[96] "O vos spiritus quorum nomina intus sunt inclusa, conjuro vos per eum cui debetis obedire principaliter, quatinus incontinenti faciatis hoc quod desidero."[97] Et sine dubio denarii illi quos expendisti revertentur ad parum tempus.

---

94 "Domine Deus omnipotens . . . die vel hora." *L* / "Domine Deus, etc." *PG*

95 Gubridali. . . . Gormi. *P* / Gubridali. Armieroch. Fratradith. Gormi. *G* / Griberi. Dali. Armierat. Fratradat. Geormi. *L* / Gubridali. Harmiteoch. Tratradeych. Corny. *Lü* / Gribridali. Harmicioc. Fratradic. Gormy. *O*

96 Et postea dic *editor* / *PL om.*

97 O vos spiritus . . . quod desidero. *L* / *P om.*

XXIX. Ut domum intrantes saltent et viriliter gaudeant

Septimadecima mansione, fac fieri annulum aureum concavum, in cujus concavitate ponantur ista nomina scripta in pergameno virgineo, scilicet:

Baratidris. Brandalia. Vertegat.[98]

Annulo completo, vade in aurora diei sequentis in introitu alicujus domus; et suffumiga dictum annulum capite inclinato cum thure, dicendo, "Domine Deus, etc." Hoc facto, tange terram cum annulo, faciendo hoc signum:

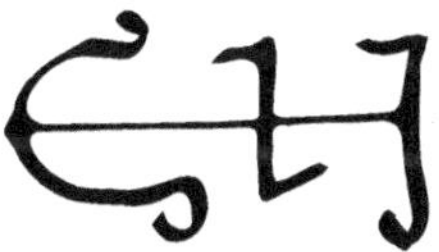

Postea involve in sindone albo. Et cum operari volueris, fac ut supra.

XXX. Experimentum verissimum ad furtum inveniendum

Octavadecima mansione, fac fieri annulum argenteum concavum et in sumitate dimittatur foramen ad modum oculi; qui oculus impleatur cera virginea et etiam modico visco querci. Die sequenti in aurora,[99] vade in introitu

98 Baratridris. Brandalia. Vertegat. *P* / Baratrides. Brandilis. Vertegat. *G* / Baratrides. Brandalia. Vectogat. *Lü*

99 in aurora *O* / *PG om.*

alicujus secrete camera; et suffumiga cum thure et aloe. Et dic ista nomina supra annulum, scilicet:

BARDIACHA. HOSTIBILIS.[100]

Postea dic, "Domine Deus omnipotens, etc., quacumque die, etc., culpabilis furti facti sentiat in oculo suo puncturam quam faciam in cera istius foraminis."[101] Et cum volueris operari, fac ut in aliis.

XXXI. UT DEMONEM PRIVATUM HABEAS QUE TIBI DICAT[102] OMNIA ET QUESITUS RESPONDEAT[103]

Nonadecima mansione, fac fieri annulum aureum non concavum, sed in eo sit scriptum hoc nomen:

MAGRADARIOTH.[104]

Et ponatur desuper allectorius.[105] Annulo completo, vade in aurora diei sequentis in introitu alicujus ville vel nemoris vel jardini; et suffumiga dictum annulum cum thure et visco querci, dicendo, "Domine Deus, etc.", sed

---

100 Bardiacha. Hostibilis. *P* / Bardiaca. Hostibilis. *G* / Bardica. Hostibilis. *Lü* / Bardiaca. Hastipru. *O*

101 Postea dic . . . istius foraminis. *editor* / Postea dic . . . facio . . . istius foraminis. *O* / Furti sciam seu fac in oculi punctura quam faciam in cera istius foraminis. *P*

102 dicat *PAG* / doceat *G*

103 respondeat *GO* / re deat *P*

104 Magradarioth. *PAGLLüO (!)*

105 allectorius *O* / altericus *P*

mutando petitionem, etc. Hoc facto, fac ut tangas terram cum annulo, faciendo hoc signum:

Hoc facto, custodi annulum mundissime in sindone nigro. Et cum operari volueris, fac ut supra.

XXXII. AD HABENDAM QUAMLIBET MULIEREM

Vicesima mansione, fac fieri annulum pulcrum argenteum concavum, in cujus concavitate includantur et ponantur ista nomina scripta in pergameno virgineo, scilicet:

HEREBRETH. FARTIGRAT. PERMISBRET. NOTH.[106]

Annulo completo, etc., in aurora diei sequentis, vade in introitu alicujus prati; et suffumiga annulum cum capillis mulieris, dicendo, "Domine Deus, etc." Et postea custodi mundissime in panno novo lineo. Et cum vis operari, fac ut in aliis.

XXXIII. AD PONENDUM MAGNAM DISCORDIAM INTER ALIQUOS

Vicesima prima mansione, fac fieri annulum plumbeum concavum, in cujus concavitate ponantur ista nomina scripta in pergameno virgineo:

106 Herebreth. . . . Noch. *P* / Hesebret. Factogret. Permilbo. Choth. *L* / Horrebreth. Fartigrar. Pernusbreth. Noth. *Lü*

BRACHALIM. FURTERHOTH. TENNUAT.[107]

Annulo completo, in aurora diei sequentis, vade in introitu alicujus latrine;[108] et suffumiga annulum cum sulfure, dicendo nomina scripta ter. Postea annulum custodi in marsupio lupi facto. Et cum volueris operari, reitera nomina ista tangendo annulum cum saliva.

XXXIV. AD PONENDUM AMICITIAM INTER ALIQUOS

Vicesima secunda mansione, fac fieri annulum aureum[109] concavum, in cujus concavitate ponantur ista nomina scripta in pergameno virgineo, scilicet:

ASTROTA. TARBIN. STAYRABANGORIATH.[110]

Annulo completo, etc., in aurora diei sequentis, vade in introitu alicujus domus; et suffumiga ipsum[111] cum thure, dicendo, "Domine Deus, etc." Et custodi ipsum in sindone rubeo novo. Et cum volueris operari, fac ut in aliis fecisti.

---

107 Brachalim. . . . Tennuat. *P* / Bracalim. Fiatant. Temiorpt. *L* / Biataliz. Furtoihot. Celatrine vel Saterne. *Lü*

108 latrine *editor* / latrine vel saterne *P*

109 aureum *L* / *P om.*

110 Astrota. . . . Stayrabangoriath. *P* / Vestiote. Tarbustaym. Vamgonatus. *L* / Astrota. Torbin. Scagraban. Goriath. *Lü*

111 et suffumiga ipsum *editor* / suffumiga eum *L* / fumiga ipsum *Lü* / *P om.*

XXXV. UT SIS INVISIBILIS

Vicesima tertia mansione, fac fieri pulverem de ossibus latronum, quem custodi in pixide argentea cum istis nominibus scriptis in pergameno virgineo, scilicet:

BUCHYFALI. CHAMARIDICH. HAUTRICATH.[112]

Hoc facto, suffumiga omnia cum pice navali. Et cum volueris operari, tradas quibus volueris, dicendo: "Domine Deus, etc.", recitando[113] semel illa nomina.

XXXVI. UT INIMICI TUI TE DILIGANT

Vicesima quarta mansione,[114] fac fieri pulverem de omnibus pilis tuis et unguibus tuis et de rasura pedum tuorum et manuum tuarum, et sanguine tui digiti minorum sinistri manus, et de stercore tuo prius ad solem desiccato;[115] et suffumiga cum thure die sequenti in aurora, dicendo ista nomina:[116]

---

112 Buchyfali. . . . Hautricath. *P* / Bictisaly. Camarideth. Hariothet. *L* / Buchifali. Chamaridach. Hantireath. *Lü*

113 "Domine Deus, etc.", recitando *editor* / "Domine Deus", recitando *L* / *P om.*

114 mansione *Lü* / *P om.*

115 stercore tuo prius ad solem desiccato *Lü* / stercore ad solem *P*

116 dicendo ista nomina *editor per cap. XXVII* / *P om.*

QUECILLA. RATIOR. CUBETO. VATULITER.[117]

Et custodi in vase vitreo. Et cum vis operari, fac ut in aliis.

XXXVII. UT EQUUS VEL ALIUD ANIMAL APPAREAT IN ACTU

Vicesima quinta mansione, fac fieri annulum stagneum concavum, in cujus concavitate ponantur ista nomina scripta in pergameno virgineo, scilicet:

GARIECH. FIRTIMELTIM. AMAMBILCH.[118]

Annulo completo, in aurora sequentis diei, perge in introitu alicujus stabuli; et suffumiga dictum annulum cum unguibus caballinis et visco querci, devote dicendo, "Domine Deus, etc." Hoc facto, custodi annulum in sindone viridi novo. Et cum volueris operari, fac ut supra.

XXXVIII. UT DENARII ALICUJUS IN FORMICAS CONVERTANTUR[119]

Vicesima sexta mansione Lune, fac fieri annulum ferreum concavum, in cujus concavitate ponantur ista nomina scripta in pergameno virgineo, scilicet:

117 Q̄cilla. Ratior. Cubeto. Vatulit~. *P* / Catilaret vel Calciaret. Jertubety. Panchalitar. *L*

118 Gariech . . . Amambilch *P* / Garior. Foromaloh. Hunambiloth vel Fortimolith. *L* / Garieth. Firmelti. Amamblith. *Lü*

119 formicas convertantur *GLLü* / formicis revertantur *P*

Satyteyr. Tornit. Hadrigar.[120]

Annulo completo, in aurora diei sequentis, perge quocumque vis; et suffumiga predictum annulum cum ovis formicarum, devote dicendo, "Domine Deus, etc." Postea tange terram cum annulo, faciendo hoc signum:

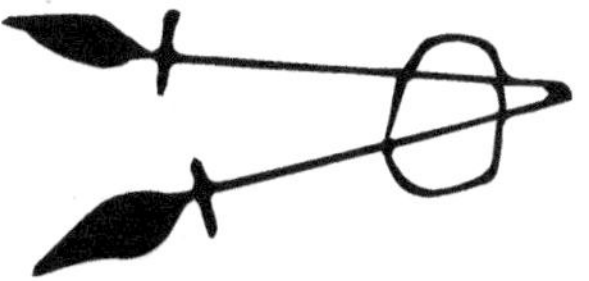

Hoc facto, custodi annulum in sindone albo. Et cum operari volueris, fac ut supra.

XXXIX. Ut formice denarii appareant

Vicesima septima mansione, fac fieri annulum plumbeum concavum, in cujus concavitate ponantur ista nomina scripta in pergameno virgineo, scilicet:

Yligar. Mancipal. Mare. Marcalia.[121]

Annulo completo, vade in aurora diei sequentis ad locum ubi sunt plurime formice; et ibi annulum suffumiga cum visco querci, dicendo devote et inclinato capite, "Domine Deus, etc." Hoc facto, custodi dictum annulum in sindone turchino. Et cum operari volueris, fac ut in

120 Satyteyr. . . . Hadrigar. *P* / Satiteir. Tornit. Adriagar. *G* / Sacassaeyt. Terayt. Obegar. *L* / Scitetie. Tor. Vivit. Sadrigar. *Lü*

121 Yligar. . . . Marcalia. *P* / Yliyar. Mancipal. Mare. Marcalium. *(?)* *G* / Lignr. Mancipal. Martalio. *L* / Hliyar. Mantipal. Mare. Marcalis. *Lü*

aliis; sed in omnibus muta petitionem quando dicitur illa oratio: "Domine Deus, etc." Hoc facto, denarii formice apparebunt.

XL. Ut de formicis thesauris gentes te facere credant

Vicesima octava et ultima mansione, fac fieri annulum aureum concavum, in cujus concavitate ponatur istud nomen scriptum in pergameno virgineo,[122] scilicet:

Doguenoyth.[123]

Annulo completo, in aurora diei sequentis, vade in introitu tue camera; et suffumiga istum annulum cum visco querci, devote dicendo, "Domine Deus, etc.", sed mutando petitionem. Hoc facto, custodi annulum in sindone nigro. Et cum volueris operari, fac ut in aliis.

Et hec sufficiant de viginti octo mansionibus Lune.

FINIS[124]

---

122 virgineo *GLü* / *P om.*

123 Doguenoyth. *P* / Doguenioth. *G* / Perecuneyth *L* / Dognenoyth *Lü*

124 Finis *GLü* / *P om.*

TRANSLATION

The Experiments of the Rings of Peter of Abano

Here happily begin the Experiments of the Rings of Peter of Abano, a most expert doctor of art and medicine, and in all sciences a most excellent master.

First and foremost in this art, it is to be considered that there are twenty-eight mansions of the Moon, each of which is given twelve degrees of the zodiac, twelve minutes and two seconds.[125]

The first mansion of the Moon is the beginning of Aries.
The second is the middle of Aries.
The third is the end of Aries.
The fourth is the beginning and middle of Taurus.
The fifth is the end of Taurus and the beginning of Gemini.
The sixth is the middle of Gemini.
The seventh is the end of Gemini.
The eighth is the beginning of Cancer.
The ninth is the middle of Cancer.
The tenth is the end of Cancer and the beginning of Leo.
The eleventh is the middle of Leo.

---

125 As often happens in texts containing numbers, the passage seems to be corrupt. An equal division of the mansions comes to twelve degrees, fifty-one minutes and approximately twenty-six seconds.

The twelfth is the end of Leo and the beginning of Virgo.
The thirteenth is the middle of Virgo.
The fourteenth is the end of Virgo.
The fifteenth is the beginning of Libra.
The sixteenth is the middle of Libra.
The seventeenth is the end of Libra and the beginning of Scorpio.
The eighteenth is the middle of Scorpio.
The nineteenth is the end of Scorpio and the beginning of Sagittarius.
The twentieth is the middle of Sagittarius.
The twenty-first is the end of Sagittarius.
The twenty-second is the beginning of Capricorn.
The twenty-third is the middle of Capricorn.
The twenty-fourth is the end of Capricorn and the beginning of Aquarius.
The twenty-fifth is the middle of Aquarius.
The twenty-sixth is the end of Aquarius and the beginning of Pisces.
The twenty-seventh is the middle of Pisces.
The twenty-eighth and last is the end of Pisces.

Here end the mansions of the Moon.

Now note that the first mansion of the Moon is said to be that through which the Moon travels over the course of a day and a night; and so run the second, the third, and the rest in like wise.

I. THAT THERE SHOULD APPEAR A RIVER IN THE AIR

In the first mansion of the Moon, cause a silvern ring to be made, in the hollow of which these names should be placed, written on virgin parchment:

PHARAI. MURATH. LAMERTHE. BAROY.

Let these names be written with the blood of an eel, and let the ring be without a stone. When the ring is complete without an opening, hold it on the following day at dawn upon the bank of some river; and thou shalt open thy mouth towards the river on bended knees, pronouncing the following orison. And do thou suffumigate the ring with incense.

Orison: "O Lord God Almighty, who from the highest heaven seest the abyss, through whom the living live and the dying die, who didst overwhelm the host of Pharaoh in the waters of the sea, and who didst raise up the spring in the desert: I beseech the bounty of thy benignity, that on whatsoever day or hour I shall have touched this ring with my spittle, these four spirits whose names are herein enclosed shall cause a marvelous river to appear, whensoever and wheresoever I will, manfully and without delay."

When this is done, touch the water with the ring, making this sign:

Having done so, enwrap the said ring in white muslin and keep it most cleanly. Now when thou wouldst operate, touch the ring with thy spittle, speaking thus:

"O ye spirits, whose names are enclosed within this ring, I conjure and adjure you by him whom firstly ye must obey, by this most sacred orison aforesaid, by all the most holy names of God, and by all the saints and saintesses of God's heavenly court, that on pain of eternal fire ye should cause the beautiful river or lake or sea of my desire to appear in such a place."

II. For the Working of the Same

Cause a ring to be made in the first mansion of the Moon as thou hast done above; but let the ring be of iron and hollowed, in the hollow of which these names should be placed on common parchment:

STORPHALUS. PARPALIN. GUROHRIT.

When the ring is complete, do thou suffumigate it with mistletoe[126] and the blood of a ram, saying, "O Lord God Almighty, etc.", as thou saidst above. This being done, touch the river with the ring. And when thou wouldst operate, speak as above, etc.

---

126 Translating an unusual term found also in the *Liber aggregationis* ascribed to Albertus Magnus, lib. I, cap. X: "The tenth herb is called by the Chaldeans *lipporax*, by the Greeks *hesifen*, by the Latins *viscus querci*. It grows on trees by boring into the tree" (pp. 277–278).

III. THAT THERE SHOULD APPEAR A STAG, AND HOUNDS PURSUING IT IN THEIR MIDST

In the second mansion of the Moon, cause a hollowed silvern ring to be made, in the hollow of which these names should be placed, written on virgin parchment with the blood of a stag and a hound mixed together:

ANNA. HEASIL. SORPHAIL. VACERAIL.

When the ring is complete and its opening stopped, hold it at dawn on the following day at the entrance of some wooded place. And thou shalt open thy mouth towards the wood, and pronounce this orison on bended knees.

Orison: "O Lord God Almighty, who from the highest heaven seest the abyss, through whom the living live and the dying die, who didst make in the world the great forests and other growing things: I beseech the bounty of thy benignity, that on whatsoever day or hour I should touch this ring with my spittle, those spirits whose names are enclosed in this ring shall cause a stag and two pursuing hounds to come forth before mine eyes or those of whomever I should wish without delay."

Having said this, touch the earth with the ring, making this sign:

This accomplished, enwrap the ring in green muslin and keep it most cleanly. Now when thou wouldst touch the ring with thy spittle, speak thus:

"O ye spirits, whose names are enclosed within this ring, I conjure and adjure you by him whom ye are bounden firstly to obey, that ye will do manfully what I desire, without delay."

When this is done, thou shalt see the stag and the hounds, and other wonders.

IV. That a Prisoner Might Be Able to Be Released from Prison and His Chains

In the second mansion of the Moon, cause a hollowed iron ring to be made, in the hollow of which these names should be placed, written on virgin parchment, to wit:

Quadra. Brimeth.

When the ring is complete, proceed to the entrance of some tower; and suffumigate the said ring with the hair of robbers, saying, "O Lord God, etc." Afterwards, touch the chains with the said ring, and without doubt thou shalt see the prisoner delivered.

V. That Armed Soldiers Should Appear

In the third mansion of the Moon, cause a hollowed golden ring to be made, in the hollow of which these names should be placed, written on virgin parchment with the blood of some man, to wit:

ANELIM. ALIBEAT. ESTADE. BOAD. BARTIFARI.

When the ring is complete, hold it on the following day at dawn at the entrance of some battlefield, and suffumigate it with the teeth of some dead man; and, facing the battlefield, pronounce the following orison.

Orison: "O Lord God Almighty, who from the highest heaven seest the deepest abysses, who hast formed man in thine image and likeness, through whom the living live and the dying die: I beseech the bounty of thy benignity, that on whatsoever day or hour I should touch this ring with my spittle, these spirits whose names are here enclosed within it shall cause armed soldiers doing battle to appear manfully before mine eyes or those of whomever I should will."

Having said this, touch the earth with the ring, making this sign:

Thereafter, enwrap the ring in black muslin and keep it most cleanly. Now when thou wouldst operate, touching the ring with thy spittle, pronounce:

"O ye spirits, whose names are herein enclosed, I conjure and adjure you by him whom ye are bounden to obey, that ye will do at once what I desire."

This done, thou shalt see soldiers doing battle, without doubt.

VI. That in One Hour Thou Mightest Be Able to Go a Hundred Miles Without Harm

In the third mansion of the Moon, cause a hollowed golden ring to be made, in the hollow of which these names should be placed, written on virgin parchment, to wit:

FARIMAN. BERGATH. BUTHATH.

When the ring is complete, go at dawn on the following day to the entrance of some wooded place; and suffumigate the said ring with mistletoe and horse-dung, saying, "O Lord God, etc.", that "the spirits whose names are enclosed within this ring might appear unto me in the form of a horse, which will carry me securely, without any harm to body or soul." But do thou neither look back nor sign thyself, while thou art upon the horse.

VII. That There Should Appear an Arbor with Fertile Branches and Vines

In the fourth mansion of the Moon, cause a hollowed golden ring to be made, in the hollow of which these names should be placed, written on virgin parchment with the ink of thorn-trees,[127] to wit:

HERADI. HATIARIE. FASTUR. CRAULYARUY.

127 A receipt for the making of such ink is given by Theophilus, *On Divers Arts* 1.38, p. 42.

When the ring is complete, hold it on the following day at dawn at the entrance of some vineyard, pronouncing these words towards the vineyard:

"O Lord God, who once changed water into wine, who from the utmost heaven seest the abyss, through whom the living live and the dying die: I beseech the bounty of thy benignity, that on whatsoever day or hour I should touch this ring with my spittle, those spirits whose names are here enclosed within it shall cause a vine adorned with clusters of grapes to appear before mine eyes wherever I will, without any delay."

When this is done, touch the earth with the ring, making this sign:

Having done so, enwrap it in green muslin and keep it most cleanly. Now when thou wouldst operate, do as with the others aforesaid.

VIII. Of Two Warring or Disputing Parties, Thou Mayest Cause the One to Prevail Whom Thou Wilt

In the fourth mansion, cause a hollowed iron ring to be made, in the hollow of which these names should be placed, written on common parchment, to wit:

FAMUAR. CHULYARIB.

On the following day, hold the said ring in thy chamber; and suffumigate it with mistletoe and with virgin wax, saying, "O Lord God, etc.", as above: speak not of the sending of the vine, but rather say, "To whomever I shall give or entrust this ring, let thy power be against his enemy; or let him emerge triumphant." This done, keep the said ring most cleanly in the whitest muslin. And when thou wouldst operate, do as thou hast done above with the others.

IX. That There Should Appear Woodlands with Forests and Green Meadows

In the fifth mansion of the Moon, cause a hollowed coppern ring to be made, in the hollow of which these names should be placed, written on virgin parchment with the blood of a green lizard, to wit:

Osturies. Bragandi. Jucamischada. Pachimisca.

When the ring is complete, hold it at dawn on the following day at the entrance of some meadow; and suffumigate the ring with hay. But speak thus with thy head bowed towards the meadow:

"O Lord God Almighty, who from the utmost heaven seest the abyss, who hast permitted the divers herbs to grow, through whom the living live and the dying die: I beseech the bounty of thy benignity, that on whatsoever day or hour I should touch this ring with my spittle, those spirits whose names are here enclosed within it shall cause beautiful woodlands with flowers and green meadows to appear before our eyes without delay, whenever and wherever I will."

This done, touch the earth with the ring, making this sign:

Thereafter, enwrap the ring in unworked linen cloth, and keep it most cleanly. And when thou wouldst operate, do as has been said.

X. That Thine Enemy, Whatsoever His Strength, Should Be Enfeebled by Infirmity

In the fifth mansion, cause a hollowed leaden ring to be made, in the hollow of which this name should be placed, written on common parchment, to wit:

Habraculith.

On the following day, hold this ring at a meeting of three ways; and on bended knees, suffumigate it with human dung, saying, "O Lord God, etc." But change the petition thus, to say that "whomever I should touch with this ring or cause to touch the same, such a one will fall ill with an infirmity, etc." Thereafter, when thou wouldst operate, touch the ring with thy spittle; and keep it most cleanly in black muslin, etc.

XI. That There Should Be Seen a Table Adorned with Abundance and Various Cloths and Meats

In the sixth mansion of the Moon, cause a hollowed tin ring to be made, in the hollow of which these names should be placed, written on virgin parchment with the blood of a cow, to wit:

BARDARI. ACER. PREDO. GAMMAGANDARVI. HASTAPULO.

When the ring is complete, etc., hold it at dawn on the following day at the entrance of some kitchen; and suffumigate it with the brain of a pig, and say with head bowed towards the kitchen:

"O Lord God Almighty, etc., from whom naught is hidden, through whom the living live and the dying die: I beseech the bounty of thy benignity, that on whatsoever day or hour I should touch this ring with my spittle, those spirits whose names are here placed within it shall cause a beautiful and abundant table adorned with divers meats to appear before our eyes without any delay, whenever and wherever I should wish."

Having said this, touch the earth with the ring, making this sign:

This done, do thou enwrap the ring in linen cloth and keep it most cleanly. Now when thou wouldst operate, do as told previously with the methods and things required.

XII. THAT ONE INFIRM SHOULD RECOVER HIS GLADNESS AND BE HEALED

In the sixth mansion of the Moon, cause a hollowed golden ring to be made, in the hollow of which these names should be placed, written on virgin parchment, to wit:

DARATEES. ESORUM. TINCHIR.

When the ring is complete, etc., suffumigate it in some chamber with incense and virgin wax, saying, "O Lord God, etc.", as written above, so that "whatsoever man or woman I should touch with this ring, or cause to touch it, will recover his or her gladness, and that such a one should be delivered from infirmity, etc." This done, keep the said ring most cleanly in azure muslin. And when thou wouldst operate, do as above.

XIII. THAT A TREE SHOULD APPEAR WITH FRUIT OR WITHOUT, AS THOU WILT

In the seventh mansion, cause a hollowed iron ring to be made, in the hollow of which these names should be placed, written on virgin parchment, to wit:

CAMBRISTAY. ANURECHA. FARASTARIO.

When the ring is complete, etc., hold it at dawn on the following day at the entrance of some tree-garden; and bowing thy head, suffumigate the said ring with aloeswood, saying, "O Lord God, etc.", and making thy desired petition as thou hast done with the others. This done, touch the earth, making these characters:

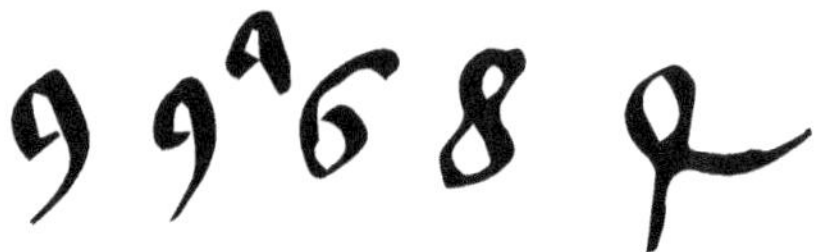

Thereafter, wrap up the ring in golden-yellow muslin. And when thou wouldst operate, do as with the others, etc.

XIV. That Those Who Eat Worms Should Appear to Eat Clusters of Grapes

In the seventh mansion, cause a hollowed tin ring to be made, in the hollow of which these names should be placed, written on common parchment, to wit:

HYERSERUS. MAURNACH. NAURSTIC.

When the ring is complete, hold it at dawn in thy chamber; and suffumigate it with little worms of the earth, saying, "O Lord God, etc.", but changing the petition, so that "whoever shall hold this ring, when worms are placed before him, by the power of these spirits here enclosed within it, let him appear to eat the clusters of the vine, whenever and wherever I will."

XV. That There Should Be Seen to Appear an Oak-tree with Divers Birds and Flowers

In the eighth mansion of the Moon, cause a ring to be made of the root of an oak-tree, on which should be written this name:

Rariath.

When the ring is complete, hold it at the entrance of an oak-grove; and suffumigate it with oak-leaves, with head bowed, saying, "O Lord God, etc.", so that "whenever or wherever I will, that spirit whose name is enclosed within it shall cause a beautiful oak-tree bedecked with divers birds and leaves fully to appear before our eyes without delay." This done, touch the earth with the ring, making this sign:

Now enwrap it in cotton wool. And when thou wouldst operate, do as before, touching the ring with thy saliva; and perform all that is required, as thou didst with the others, etc.

XVI. That Those Who Eat Clusters of Grapes Should Appear to Eat Worms

In the eighth mansion, cause a hollowed silvern ring to be made, in the hollow of which this name should be placed, written on virgin paper, to wit:

SAUFAOLE.

On the following day, etc., at dawn, suffumigate it in some field with grapes, saying, "O Lord God, etc.", but changing the petition to say, "Whoever shall hold this ring, when clusters of grapes are placed before him, by the power of this spirit here enclosed within it, let him appear to eat terrestrial worms, whenever and wherever I will." And when thou wouldst operate, do as with the others, etc.

XVII. That There Should Be Seen a Mouse Dragging a Millstone behind It

In the ninth mansion, cause a hollowed silvern ring to be made, in the hollow of which these names should be placed, written on virgin parchment, to wit:

TRELLARI. YENUAT. BOURNES. BOURNAY. SYETH.

When the ring is complete, etc., at dawn on the following day, go to the entrance of some millhouse; and suffumigate it with wheat, saying, "O Lord God, etc.", but changing the petition, so that "those spirits whose names are here enclosed within it will by their power cause a mouse dragging a millstone behind it to appear before our eyes, on pain of eternal fire, etc." This done, touch the earth near the edge of the water of the mill with the ring, making this sign:

Having done so, enwrap the said ring in the skin of a mouse and keep it most cleanly. And when thou wouldst operate, do as with the others, etc.

XVIII. That a Man of Whatsoever Sort Should Abandon His House and Flee

In the ninth mansion, cause a hollowed leaden ring to be made, in the hollow of which these names should be placed, written on virgin parchment, to wit:

Jeartaag. Bellicorth. Sirgith.

But on the following day, suffumigate it with brimstone in a privy, saying the aforesaid names thrice. Then touch the earth with the ring, etc. And when thou wouldst operate, do as above with the others, etc.

XIX. That There Should Appear a Bed with Pillows, Linens, and Other Fair Adornments

In the tenth mansion of the Moon, cause a hollowed golden ring to be made, in the hollow of which these names should be placed, written on common parchment, to wit:

Bernerecha. Baxo. Monego. Difinicha.

When the ring is complete, go at dawn on the following day to the entrance of some bed-chamber, and suffumigate the said ring with new cloths, saying with head bowed, "O Lord God, etc.", so that "those spirits whose names are enclosed within this ring shall cause by their power a beautiful bed adorned with all adornments to appear manfully before our eyes and those of whomever I will, on pain of eternal fire, etc." This done, touch the earth with the ring, making this sign:

Thereafter, enwrap it in some piece of newly-wrought linen cloth. And when thou wouldst operate, do as above.

XX. THAT THOU SHOULDST BE ABLE SKILLFULLY TO FIND HIDDEN TREASURE

In the tenth mansion, cause a hollowed golden ring to be made, in the hollow of which this name should be placed, written on virgin parchment, to wit:

HEUSENEBIOR.

On the following day, suffumigate it in thy chamber at dawn with fennel and incense, saying, "O Lord God, etc." Now put the said ring beneath thy head when thou sleepest, and thou shalt see in a dream where there be treasure. Keep it most cleanly in turquoise-colored muslin; and when thou wouldst operate, speak and do as with the others.

XXI. THAT THERE SHOULD APPEAR MANFULLY AN ELEPHANT BEARING A CASTLE

In the eleventh mansion, cause an ivory ring to be made, not hollowed, but there being this name written on its sides, to wit:

FERNAGITIM.

When the ring is complete, go at dawn on the following day to the entrance of some castle; and suffumigate the said ring with ivory and the hair of living men, saying, "O Lord God, etc.", but changing the petition, so that "that spirit whose name is marked upon this ring shall cause by its power a marvelous elephant to appear bearing a castle, etc." This done, touch the earth with the ring, making this sign:

Having done so, keep the said ring most cleanly in an ivory casket. And when thou wouldst operate, do as with the others.

XXII. That a House or Estate Should Appear to Be Visibly Burning

In the eleventh mansion, cause a hollowed golden ring to be made, in the hollow of which these names should be placed, written on virgin parchment, to wit:

GARIDOLICALU. FURINICAT. BRACHUCAL.

At dawn on the following day, suffumigate it at the entrance of some estate or house, saying, "O Lord God, etc.", so that "whatsoever house or estate one shall have gone round with this ring, those spirits whose names are here enclosed in it shall cause by their power that house or estate to seem to burn manfully to those who behold it." This done, keep the ring most cleanly in any clean place.

XXIII. That There Should Appear a Great and Horrible Serpent[128]

In the twelfth mansion, cause a hollowed coppern ring to be made, in the hollow of which these names should be placed, written on common parchment, to wit:

DOMINATH. BORIATIACALI. ENAPRIA. TERIATH.

When the ring is complete, go at dawn on the following day to the entrance of some meadow, and

128 Alternatively, "Dragon".

suffumigate it with the blood of a serpent,[129] saying, "O Lord God, etc." This done, touch the earth with the ring, making this sign:

Thereafter, keep it in unworked white linen cloth. And when thou wouldst operate, do as above.

XXIV. That Thou Mightest Cause Whomever Thou Wilt to Take Off His Garments

In the twelfth mansion, cause a hollowed tin ring to be made, in the hollow of which this name should be placed, written on virgin parchment, to wit:

DORDRACHUTH.

On the following day at dawn, suffumigate it on a public street with the blood of a he-goat, saying, "O Lord God, etc.", so that "whoever, etc." Now do as with the others.

129 Alternatively, "dragon's blood". While it is true that Peter of Abano's accepted writings employ this term in the modern sense of a type of resin (see for example *Conciliator*, diff. CXC, f. 245v, E), that interpretation seems unlikely here, given the use of various kinds of animal blood throughout.

XXV. That There Should Appear a Spring or a Well upon a Field or in a Chamber

In the thirteenth mansion of the Moon, cause a hollowed tin ring to be made, in the hollow of which should be written these names, to wit:

RODER. PACORP.

When the ring is complete, go at dawn on the following day to the mouth of some spring or well; and there suffumigate the ring with water, saying, "O Lord God, etc." This done, touch any stone of the mouth, making this sign:

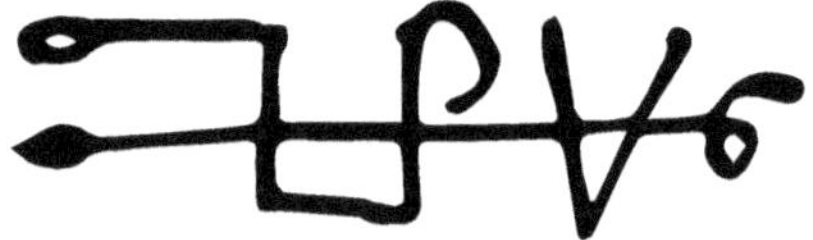

Having done so, keep it in a vessel filled with clear water. And when thou wouldst operate, do as above.

XXVI. That There Should Appear a Castle with Its Appurtenances in Whatever Place Thou Wilt

In the fourteenth mansion, cause a hollowed ring to be made, in the hollow of which these names should be placed, written on virgin parchment, to wit:

GORALIDIO. BRANDAMIROTH. SCAURIOCI.

When the ring is complete, go at dawn on the following day to the entrance of some castle; and suffumigate the said ring with quicklime, saying, "O Lord God, etc." This done, touch the earth with the ring, making this sign:

Thereafter, enwrap it in black linen cloth, etc. And when thou wouldst operate, do as above.

XXVII. That a Moving Mountain Should Seem to Approach a House

In the fifteenth mansion, cause a powder to be made of the blood of a serpent, aloe, and mistletoe. At dawn on the following day, bring this powder near some mountain; and suffumigate it with the earth of the same or another mountain, pronouncing these names:

TERTIN. MODA. BRASILIR. GODRIR. BODRE.

Then say, "O Lord God, etc." This done, keep the said powder in a silvern casket. And when thou wouldst operate, sprinkle the powder, as before.

XXVIII. That the Coins Which Thou Hast Spent Should Return unto Thee

In the sixteenth mansion of the Moon, take coins of whatever sort thou wilt and tie them up in new golden-yellow muslin. Now suffumigate the whole of this with mistletoe, saying:

"O Lord God Almighty, who from the utmost heaven seest the abysses, who hast formed men in thine image and likeness, through whom the living live and the dying die: I beseech the bounty of thy benignity, that on whatsoever day or hour I should touch this golden muslin with my spittle, these spirits whose names are enclosed within it shall cause the coins to return to me with their companions at any day or hour."

And when thou wouldst spend them, pronounce these names most secretly:

GUBRIDALI. HARMUROCH. FRATRADRITH. GORMI.

Then say: "O ye spirits whose names are herein enclosed, I conjure you by him whom ye are bounden firstly to obey, that ye will do this which I desire at once." And without doubt, those coins which thou hast spent will return in a short time.

XXIX. That Those Who Enter a House Should Dance and Rejoice Manfully

In the seventeenth mansion, cause a hollowed golden ring to be made, in the hollow of which these names should be placed, written on virgin parchment, to wit:

BARATIDRES. BRANDALIA. VERTEGAT.

When the ring is complete, go at dawn on the following day to the entrance of some house; and suffumigate the said ring with incense, saying with bowed head, "O Lord God, etc." This done, touch the earth with the ring, making this sign:

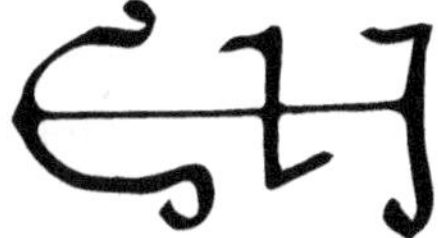

Thereafter, enwrap it in white muslin. And when thou wouldst operate, do as above.

XXX. A Most Veracious Experiment for the Discovery of Theft

In the eighteenth mansion, cause a hollowed silvern ring to be made, leaving an opening on top in the shape of an eye; and let this eye be filled up with virgin wax and a little mistletoe withal. On the following day at dawn, go to the entrance of some secret chamber; and suffumigate it with incense and aloe. And pronounce these names over the ring, to wit:

BARDIACHA. HOSTIBILIS.

Then say, "O Lord God almighty, etc., on whatsoever day, etc., let him who is guilty of the theft feel in his eye the pricking which I shall make in the wax of this aperture." And when thou wouldst operate, do as with the others.

XXXI. That Thou Shouldst Have a Private Daemon That Will Tell Thee Everything and Answer When Besought

In the nineteenth mansion, cause a golden ring to be made, not hollowed, but there being written upon it this name:

MAGRADARIOTH.

And let an allectorius[130] be laid thereon. When the ring is complete, go at dawn on the following day to the entrance of some estate or wood or garden; and suffumigate the said ring with incense and mistletoe, saying, "O Lord God, etc.", but changing the petition, etc. This done, do thou touch the earth with the ring, making this sign:

Having done so, keep the ring most cleanly in black muslin. And when thou wouldst operate, do as above.

130 "Allectorius is a stone found in the bellies of capons, being the size of a bean and having the appearance of Crystal or clear water."—Damigeron, *De lapidibus* 3.19, p. 27. It is not difficult to see how this might have turned into the mere "crystal" enclosing Peter of Abano's legendary familiars.

XXXII. In Order to Have Whatsoever Woman

In the twentieth mansion, cause a hollowed and beauteous silvern ring to be made, in the hollow of which these names should be placed and enclosed, written on virgin parchment, to wit:

Herebreth. Fartigrat. Permisbret. Noth.

When the ring is complete, etc., at dawn on the following day, go to the entrance of some meadow; and suffumigate it with the hair of a woman, saying, "O Lord God, etc." Thereafter, keep it most cleanly in new linen cloth. And when thou wouldst operate, do as with the others.

XXXIII. For the Imposition of a Great Discord among Any

In the twenty-first mansion, cause a hollowed leaden ring to be made, in the hollow of which these names should be placed, written on virgin parchment:

Brachalim. Furterhoth. Tennuat.

When the ring is complete, go at dawn on the following day to the entrance of any privy; and suffumigate the ring with brimstone, pronouncing thrice the written names. Thereafter, keep the ring in a pouch made of wolf-skin. And when thou wouldst operate, repeat these names while touching the ring with thy spittle.

XXXIV. For the Imposition of Love among Any

In the twenty-second mansion, cause a hollowed golden ring to be made, in the hollow of which these names should be placed, written on virgin parchment, to wit:

ASTROTA. TARBIN. STAYRABANGORIATH.

When the ring is complete, etc., go at dawn on the following day to the entrance of some house; and suffumigate it with incense, saying, "O Lord God, etc." Now keep it in new red muslin. And when thou wouldst operate, do as thou hast done with the others.

XXXV. That Thou Mightest Be Invisible

In the twenty-third mansion, cause a powder to be made of the bones of robbers, which thou shalt keep in a silvern casket with these names written on virgin parchment, to wit:

BUCHYFALI. CHAMARIDICH. HAUTRICATH.

This done, suffumigate the whole with ship's tar. Now when thou wouldst operate, entrust it to whomever thou wilt, saying, "O Lord God, etc.", and reciting those names a single time.

XXXVI. That Thine Enemies Should Love Thee

In the twenty-fourth mansion, cause a powder to be made from all thy hair and nails, from the shavings of thy feet and hands, from the blood of the little finger of thy left hand, and from thine ordure previously dried in the sun; and suffumigate it with incense at dawn on the following day, pronouncing these names:

Quecilla. Ratior. Cubeto. Vatuliter.[131]

Now keep it in a glassen vessel. And when thou wouldst operate, do as with the others.

XXXVII. That There Should Appear a Horse or Other Animal in Motion

In the twenty-fifth mansion, cause a hollowed tin ring to be made, in the hollow of which these names should be placed, written on virgin parchment, to wit:

Gariech. Firtimeltim. Amambilch.

When the ring is complete, proceed on the following day at dawn to the entrance of some stable; and suffumigate the said ring with horse-hooves and mistletoe, saying devoutly, "O Lord God, etc." This done, keep the ring in new green muslin. And when thou wouldst operate, do as above.

131 These names are abbreviated in the MS and probably corrupt.

XXXVIII. That Anyone's Coins Should Be Turned into Ants

In the twenty-sixth mansion of the Moon, cause a hollowed iron ring to be made, in the hollow of which these names should be placed, written on virgin parchment, to wit:

SATYTEYR. TORNIT. HADRIGAR.

When the ring is complete, proceed at dawn on the following day whithersoever thou wilt; and suffumigate the aforesaid ring with ant-eggs, saying devoutly, "O Lord God, etc." Then touch the earth with the ring, making this sign:

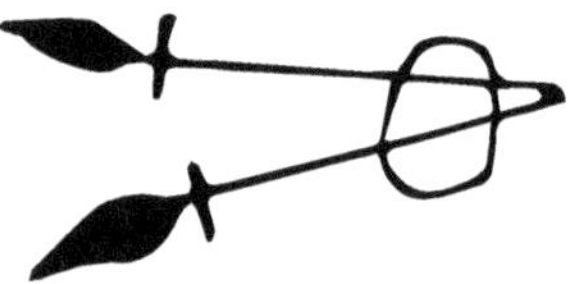

This done, keep the ring in white muslin. And when thou wouldst operate, do as above.

XXXIX. That Ants Might Appear to Be Coins

In the twenty-seventh mansion, cause a hollowed leaden ring to be made, in the hollow of which these names should be placed, written on virgin parchment, to wit:

YLIGAR. MANCIPAL. MARE. MARCALIA.

When the ring is complete, go at dawn on the following day to a place where there be very many ants;

and there suffumigate the ring with mistletoe, saying devoutly with bowed head, "O Lord God, etc." This done, keep the said ring in turquoise-colored muslin. And when thou wouldst operate, do as with the others; but in all things change the petition when thou sayest that orison: "O Lord God, etc." This done, ants will appear to be coins.

XL. That Men Should Believe Thee to Produce Treasures from Ants

In the twenty-eighth and final mansion, cause a hollowed golden ring to be made, in the hollow of which this name should be placed, written on virgin parchment, to wit:

DOGUENOYTH.

When the ring is complete, go at dawn on the following day to the entrance of thy chamber, and suffumigate this ring with mistletoe, saying devoutly, "O Lord God, etc.", but changing the petition. This done, keep the ring in black muslin. And when thou wouldst operate, do as with the others.

Now concerning the twenty-eight mansions of the Moon, let these suffice.

FINIS

APPENDIX I

The Characters as Shown in the Manuscripts

I.
That There Should Appear a River in the Air

The Paris Manuscript

The Augsburg Manuscript

The Ghent Manuscript

The London Manuscript

The Lübeck Manuscript

III.
That There Should Appear a Stag, and Hounds Pursuing It in Their Midst

The Paris Manuscript

The Augsburg Manuscript

The Ghent Manuscript

The London Manuscript

The Lübeck Manuscript

V.
That Armed Soldiers Should Appear

The Paris Manuscript

The Ghent Manuscript

The London Manuscript

The Lübeck Manuscript

VII.
That There Should Appear an Arbor with Fertile Branches and Vines

The Paris Manuscript The London Manuscript

The Lübeck Manuscript

IX.
That There Should Appear Woodlands with Forests and Green Meadows

The Paris Manuscript The London Manuscript

The Lübeck Manuscript

XI.
That There Should Be Seen a Table Adorned with Abundance and Various Cloths and Meats

The Paris Manuscript

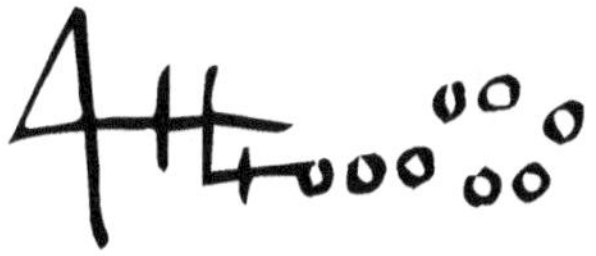

The Ghent Manuscript

The London Manuscript

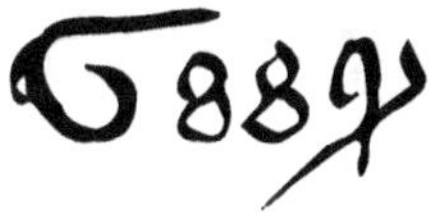

The Lübeck Manuscript

XIII.
That a Tree Should Appear with Fruit or without, as Thou Wilt

The Paris Manuscript

The Ghent Manuscript

The London Manuscript

The Lübeck Manuscript

XV.
That There Should Be Seen to Appear an Oak-tree with Divers Birds and Flowers

The Paris Manuscript

The Ghent Manuscript

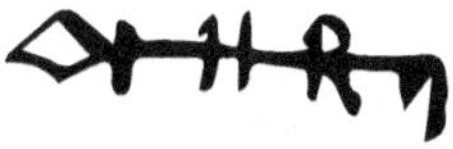

The London Manuscript

The Lübeck Manuscript

XVII.
THAT THERE SHOULD BE SEEN A MOUSE DRAGGING A MILLSTONE BEHIND IT

The Paris Manuscript

The Ghent Manuscript

The London Manuscript

The Lübeck Manuscript

XIX.
That There Should Appear a Bed with Pillows, Linens, and Other Fair Adornments

The Paris Manuscript

The Ghent Manuscript

The London Manuscript

The Lübeck Manuscript

XXI.
That There Should Appear Manfully an Elephant Bearing a Castle

The Paris Manuscript

The Ghent Manuscript

The London Manuscript

The Lübeck Manuscript

XXIII.
That There Should Appear a Great and Horrible Serpent

The Paris Manuscript

The Ghent Manuscript

The London Manuscript

The Lübeck Manuscript

XXV.
That There Should Appear a Spring or a Well upon a Field or in a Chamber

The Paris Manuscript

The Ghent Manuscript

The Lübeck Manuscript

XXVI.
That There Should Appear a Castle with Its Appurtenances in Whatever Place Thou Wilt

The Paris Manuscript

The Ghent Manuscript

The London Manuscript

The Lübeck Manuscript

XXIX.
THAT THOSE WHO ENTER A HOUSE SHOULD DANCE AND REJOICE MANFULLY

The Paris Manuscript

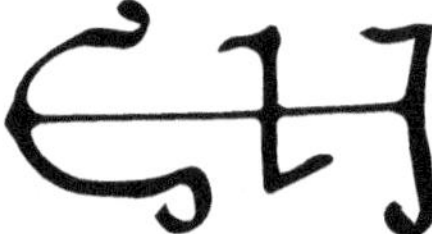

The Ghent Manuscript

The Lübeck Manuscript

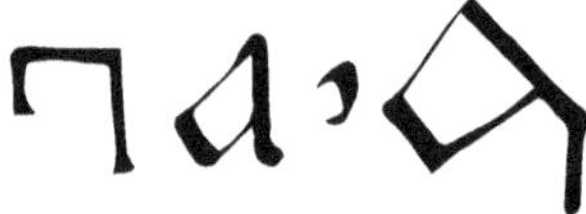

XXXI.
That Thou Shouldst Have a Private Daemon That Will Tell Thee Everything and Answer When Besought

The Paris Manuscript

The Augsburg Manuscript

The London Manuscript

The Lübeck Manuscript

The Oxford Manuscript, Ver. I

The Oxford Manuscript, Ver. II

XXXVIII.
THAT ANYONE'S COINS SHOULD BE TURNED INTO ANTS

The Paris Manuscript

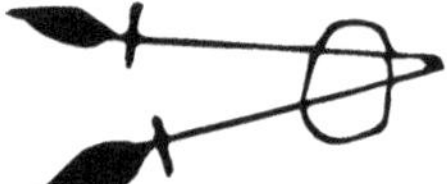

The Ghent Manuscript

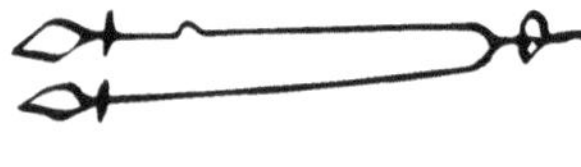

The London Manuscript

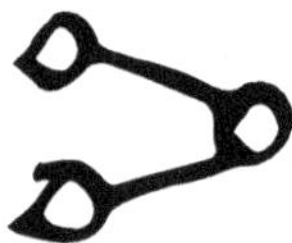

The Lübeck Manuscript

APPENDIX II

Anelli di Pietro d'Abano

There follows our translation of a short tract in the Italian vernacular, whose apparent basis in the Latin *Experimenta* merits its inclusion in the present volume. Despite the similarity of certain chapter headings, the differences are such as to mark this an original work in its own right, rather than a translation or adaptation. The text is found in a single manuscript of the fifteenth and sixteenth centuries, Florence, Biblioteca Nazionale Centrale, MS Palatino 1022, ff. 188r–191r; and in an edition of the same by Stefano Rapisarda (printed in Boudet, pp. 287–291). We have generally adhered to this edition for the present translation, indicating the necessary departures in our notes. The characters are given as they appear in the manuscript. We should make mention as well of a shorter French reworking based on the present tract (or a lost common antecessor), entitled *Les Talismans ou caracteres des douze anneaux.*[132]

132 For a translation of the *Douze Anneaux*, see Skinner, pp. 264–272. This text has been useful in clarifying doubtful passages of the *Anelli*.

THE RINGS OF PETER OF ABANO

Whereby Marvelous Experiments are Performed and Recalled in Our Day

I. THE FIRST RING

To Produce a Stag Pursued by a Multitude of Hounds without Harm

In the thirteenth mansion of the Moon, thou shalt make a hollowed coppern ring, and cause a stone of steel[133] to be laid therein, graven with this character:

Then take virgin paper, whereon thou shalt write the following name with the blood of a dove:

DALEF.

133 *pietra di acciaro*. According to the *Douze Anneaux*, the stone is lazuli (Skinner, p. 265), which seems more likely given that no other metals are used as "stones".

And thou shalt place it in the hollow of the ring, enclosing it within, and pronouncing the orison and conjuration found in the second ring,[134] saying: "O Dalef, when I shall make this sign upon the earth, let it be at once that there should appear a stag pursued by hounds in the sight of all near by", and making this sign:

It will appear at once, and will disappear when undone. Thou shalt suffumigate this with aloeswood.

134 Corrected. The MS reads "the fifth ring", an obvious error.

II. THE SECOND RING
To Have a Woman in One's Power

In the fourteenth mansion of the Moon, thou shalt cause a hollowed coppern ring to be made, wherein thou shalt set a garnet on which this sign should be graven:

Then thou shalt write on virgin paper:

ASMOLIOR.

Thou shalt enclose it in the hollow of the ring; and, holding it in thy hand, thou shalt pronounce the following orison and conjuration.[135]

135 Here follows the only portion of the tract not in the vernacular. The Latin text below is our own transcription, that of Rapisarda being defective.

Oratio: "O Domine Deus, qui ex nihilo cuncta creasti antequam fierent, gloria et honore nos coronasti, et constituisti nos super opera manuum tuarum: et omnia subjecisti sub pedibus nostris, oves et boves universas, insuper et pecora campi:[136] hoc sanctissimum verbum sit semper benedictum, per omnia saecula saeculorum. Amen, amen, amen."	Orison: "O Lord God, who created all things from naught before they were made, thou hast crowned us with glory and honor, and hast set us over the works of thy hands: thou hast subjected all things under our feet, all sheep and oxen, and moreover the beasts of the field: blessed be this most holy word forever, for all the ages of ages. Amen, amen, amen."

CONJURATION: "O Asmolior, I conjure thee by that omnipotent name which hath granted me authority, set me over the works of his hands, and crowned me with glory and honor; by the tremendous Aglator; and by that name which thou art come to obey: so that forthwith when I shall make this sign upon the earth, thou wilt cause a woman to appear who shall do all that I will." And when thou wilt that she should appear, do thou make this sign upon the earth:

136 The phrase *et pecora campi*, missing from the text, is supplied from Psalm 8:6–8 (Vulgate), on which much of this prayer is based.

And when thou wilt that she should disappear, undo the sign. On the second day, when thou shalt have operated, suffumigate this with aloeswood.

III. The Third Ring

To Make a Horse Appear, Which Will Take Thee where Thou Wilt without Harm

In the third mansion of the Moon, thou shalt make a tin ring with a black stone from the head[137] having this character:

And thou shalt write upon virgin paper:

Capriot.

And thou shalt enclose it as aforesaid; then pronounce the orison and conjuration, saying, "O Capriot, when I shall make this sign upon the earth, cause there to appear a horse without trepidation." The sign is this:

And when thou wilt that it should disappear, undo the sign. Thou shalt suffumigate this with the hair of thy head.

---

137 *pietra nera dal capo*. Something seems to be missing here. Cf. the cock-stone called radaim. "It is a black and translucent stone found in the head of a cock when it is given to ants to eat. Being borne, it avails in obtaining whatever one asks."—Arnoldus Saxo, *De virtutibus lapidum* 68, p. 443.

IV. THE FOURTH RING

To Have a Spouse Who Will Obey Thee

In the fifth mansion of the Moon, thou shalt make a silvern ring wherein thou shalt impress this sign upon a yellow stone:

And thou shalt write this name upon virgin paper:

ASTAROT.

And thou shalt enclose it as usual in the said ring; then pronounce the orison and conjuration, saying, "O Astarot, when I shall make this sign upon the earth, do thou cause a spouse to appear, who shall do all that I will." The sign is this:[138]

And when thou wilt that it should disappear, undo the sign. Thou shalt suffumigate this with amber.

138 The second appearance of the sign, supplied from above, is omitted from the MS.

V. THE FIFTH RING

To Cause a Person to Be Infirm

In the twelfth mansion of the Moon, thou shalt make a hollowed leaden ring with a black stone having this sigil engraven:

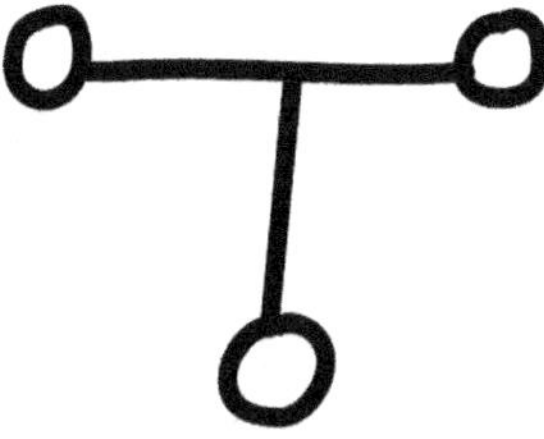

And thou shalt write this name upon virgin paper:

JURBISCACH.

And thou shalt enclose it in the ring, pronouncing the orison and conjuration, saying, "O Jurbiscach, when I shall make this sign upon the earth with this ring, let N. be ever ill with great anguish." And when thou wilt that he should recover, undo the sign. Thou shalt suffumigate this with asafetida.

VI. The Sixth Ring
To Heal One of Every Affliction

In the fifth mansion of the Moon, thou shalt make a silvern ring with a red gem having this sigil:

Thou shalt write upon virgin paper:

BALSAMIACH.

And thou shalt enclose it in the ring, pronouncing the orison and conjuration as above, saying: "O Balsamiach, when I shall make this sign upon the earth with this ring—

—do thou cause N. to be healed of his affliction." Now take care to do this in a place where it will not undo itself, for the affliction will return. Thou shalt suffumigate this with incense.

VIII. The Eighth Ring[139]
To Liberate One Possessed

In the seventh mansion of the Moon, thou shalt make a silvern ring with a gem of crystal, which thou art to engrave with this sign:

And thou shalt write this name upon virgin paper:

Cabruach.[140]

Thou shalt pronounce the wonted orison and conjuration, saying: "O Cabruach, when I shall make this sign upon the earth—

—let N. be freed from the unclean spirits." Thou shalt suffumigate this with myrrh.

---

139 The chapters appear thus out of order in the MS.

140 Per the MS. Rapisarda reads both instances of this as "Sabruach."

IX. The Ninth Ring

To Restore the Sight to Whomever Has Lost It

In the ninth mansion of the Moon, thou shalt make a silvern ring with a gem of white agate, fashioning upon it this sign:

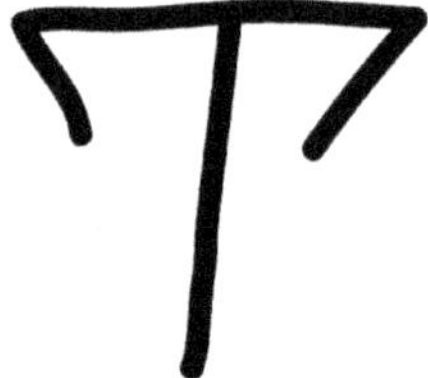

And thou shalt write this name upon virgin paper:

SALAFACH.

Thou shalt pronounce the orison and conjuration, saying: "O Salafach, when I shall make this sign upon the earth, do thou cause N. to possess his former sight." Suffumigate this with . . . seed.[141]

141 "This must be perfumed with henbane."—*Douze Anneaux* 8 (Skinner, p. 268).

VII. The Seventh Ring

To Obtain Every Favor from a Prince

In the first mansion of the Moon, thou shalt make a silvern ring with a white gem, fashioning upon it this sign:

Thou shalt write upon virgin paper:

Illusiabo.

And thou shalt enclose it as above, saying: "O Illusiabo, when I shall make this sign upon the earth with this ring, do thou cause N. to do me such a service." Then, without undoing the sign, depart unto him. The sign is this:

Thou shalt perfume this with amber.

X. THE TENTH RING

To Go Invisible

In the fourth mansion of the Moon, thou shalt make a golden ring with a red gem, impressing upon it this sign:

Then write this name upon virgin paper:

JENUCH.

Pronounce the orison and conjuration as above, saying: "O Jenuch, when I shall make this sign upon the earth, do thou render me invisible to all sight." And make this sign:

And when thou wouldst be seen, thou shalt undo it. Suffumigate this with orange peels.

XI. The Eleventh Ring

To Overcome One's Enemies

In the fourth mansion of the Moon, thou shalt make a golden ring and grave this sign thereon:

Thou shalt write this name upon virgin paper:

Jopinach.[142]

And thou shalt pronounce as above: "O Jopinach, when I shall make this sign upon the earth, do thou cause me to overcome mine enemies." Thou shalt suffumigate this with amber.

142 Per the MS. Rapisarda reads this as "Cofinach", and the second occurrence as "Jopoinach".

XII. The Twelfth Ring

To See in a Dream What Thou Wilt

In the fourteenth mansion of the Moon, thou shalt make a silvern ring with a gem of emerald, bearing this sign:

Thou shalt write this name upon virgin paper:

BELSIAR.

And thou shalt pronounce the conjuration and orison, saying: "O Belsiar, when I shall make this sign upon the earth—

—do thou cause such a thing to come by night in a dream", and name what thou wilt. Thou shalt suffumigate this with the bone of a hanged thief.

XIII. The Thirteenth Ring
To Heal Thy Horses of Every Affliction

In the twenty-second mansion of the Moon, thou shalt make a tin ring with a turquoise stone, bearing this sign:

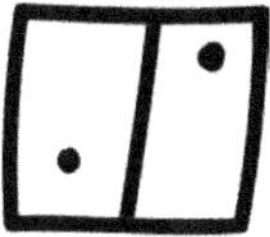

Thou shalt write this name upon virgin paper:

Anasach.

And thou shalt pronounce the orison and conjuration, saying: "O Anasach, when I shall make this sign upon the earth—

—let my horse be healed of every affliction." Undo the sign. Thou shalt suffumigate this with asafetida.

XIV. The Fourteenth Ring
To Catch a Great Quantity of Fish

In the sixteenth mansion of the Moon, thou shalt make a tin ring with a gem of glass, whereon should be this sign:

Thou shalt write upon virgin paper:

SALBUCH.

And thou shalt pronounce and say as above: "[O Salbuch,] when I shall make this sign upon the earth, mayest thou never cease from catching such kinds of fish." Undo the sign at thy pleasure. Thou shalt perfume this with aloeswood.

XV. The Fifteenth Ring

To Catch a Great Quantity of Birds

In the fifteenth mansion of the Moon, thou shalt make a coppern ring with a stone of jasper whereon thou shalt impress[143] this sign:

Thou shalt write this name upon virgin parchment:

Rampetuch.

And thou shalt pronounce as above: "O Rampetuch, when I shall make this sign upon the earth, mayest thou never cease from catching such a kind of birds or beasts." Undo it at thy pleasure. Thou shalt suffumigate this with asafetida.

Here end the Fifteen Rings of Peter of Abano.

Take heed that the operations be performed in a pure place, wearing the cleanest of garments; and pronounce the conjurations and suffumigate withal.

143 *impronterai*, per the MS. Rapisarda: *infronterai*.

APPENDIX III

Extracts from the *Picatrix*

We include this final appendix for the sake of reference and, if needed, as a guidepost to further study. Though it deals with the making of images, we think the potential application to the workings of the *Annulorum experimenta* will be seen readily enough. The following passages are translated anew from the Latin *Picatrix*, edited by David Pingree, pp. 8–15.

Picatrix, Lib. I, Cap. IV

On General Considerations and the Arrangement of the Heavens for Making Images

When the wise men of old wanted to make images, they could not set aside the constellations, which are the roots in the science of images and the means whereby their effects are brought forth. Turn we now, then, to speak of the roots of these constellations, wherewith thou wilt aid thyself in all the operations of images; and these roots will be the work of heaven for the images' effects.

But those who seek to make images must first possess a knowledge of the equations of the planets and other stars, as well as the movements of the heavens. Moreover, they must believe firmly in the operations they perform with the images, so that what they do shall be genuine and without doubt. And neither let them be in doubt concerning the effects of the same, nor let them act for the purpose of testing or proving whether they be or be not true. But rather let them hold these things to be true according to their will. The rational spirit will be reinforced hereby, and directed to that power of the higher world from which the spirit of that agency in the image proceeds. Then what is sought will come to pass.

Now, however, I would teach thee one thing which is most necessary for these operations; and this is to work when conditions are best around the world. For I say to thee, that thou shouldst do naught in these operations unless the Moon stands in a degree suitable and appropriate to the works thou wouldst perform, inasmuch as the Moon has powers and manifest workings in these lower things, which lie hidden to none.

Translator's note: The text continues here with a lengthy list of operations pertaining to the mansions of the Moon. For our purpose, however, it suffices to give a table of the longitudes, followed by the remainder of the chapter.

The Boundaries of the Twenty-eight Mansions According to the *Picatrix*, Lib. I, Cap. IV

I	♈ 00° 00’ 01” – ♈ 12° 51’ 26”
II	♈ 12° 51’ 26” – ♈ 25° 42’ 52”
III	♈ 25° 42’ 52” – ♉ 08° 34’ 02”
IV	♉ 08° 34’ 02” – ♉ 21° 25’ 44”
V	♉ 21° 25’ 44” – ♊ 04° 17’ 10”
VI	♊ 04° 17’ 10” – ♊ 17° 08’ 36”
VII	♊ 17° 08’ 36” – ♊ End
VIII	♋ 00° 00’ 01” – ♋ 12° 51’ 26”
IX	♋ 12° 51’ 26” – ♋ 25° 42’ 51”
X	♋ 25° 42’ 51” – ♌ 08° 34’ 18”
XI	♌ 08° 34’ 18” – ♌ 21° 25’ 44”
XII	♌ 21° 25’ 44” – ♍ 04° 17’ 06”
XIII	♍ 04° 17’ 06” – ♍ 17° 08’ 36”
XIV	♍ 17° 08’ 36” – ♍ End
XV	♎ 00° 00’ 01” – ♎ 12° 51’ 26”
XVI	♎ 12° 51’ 26” – ♎ 25° 42’ 52”
XVII	♎ 25° 42’ 52” – ♏ 08° 36’ 02”
XVIII	♏ 08° 36’ 02” – ♏ 21° 25’ 44”
XIX	♏ 21° 25’ 44” – ♐ 04° 17’ 10”
XX	♐ 04° 17’ 10” – ♐ 17° 08’ 46”
XXI	♐ 17° 08’ 46” – ♐ End
XXII	♑ 00° 00’ 01” – ♑ 12° 51’ 26”

XXIII	♑ 12° 51' 26" – ♑ 25° 42' 52"
XXIV	♑ 25° 42' 52" – ♒ 08° 34' 28"
XXV	♒ 08° 34' 28" – ♒ 21° 25' 44"
XXVI	♒ 21° 25' 44" – ♓ 04° 17' 10"
XXVII	♓ 04° 17' 10" – ♓ 17° 08' 36"
XXVIII	♓ 17° 08' 36" – ♓ End

Now the wise men of India kept these twenty-eight mansions as the root of all their operations and elections.

And the root hereof is that thou shalt observe in all operations for good that the Moon be safe from Saturn and Mars and their aspects, as well as from the combustion of the Sun, and that it be joined to the fortunes by good aspects, namely, a trine or sextile aspect. See to it in all these matters, that the Moon separates from one fortune and applies to another. But do contrariwise in all operations for evil.

Furthermore, it is needful that the operator in the magical art should be one who believes in his acts without any misgiving of the work. For this is the disposition of an operator who is well-disposed to receive the aforesaid works and virtues from what he intends to effect. And such a disposition, that is, a disposition of this kind, cannot be found other than in man; but the disposition which exists in other sensible things is the means whereby they receive the sensibility of their own natures—even as wax so easily receives the forms impressed upon it—and the means whereby a daemoniac receives a daemon by another's power, his body being disposed to receive such a daemon, and this because of the debility of his members and the impotence for making resistance thereto. In like wise, a disposition of debility is found in a place of strength, whereby that disposition comes to be which is needful in the things from which images are composed; for all things are disposed to receive some sort of work which conforms to them. This is the root in these operations, and all are in agreement about them. When there is a disposition to receive such things, the reception will be made; and when there is a reception, the work will be patent and manifest, and the figure will receive its strength. And it shall be the work which thou seekest, insofar as matter and form are joined together as one: even as the figure of a man is united with a mirror and water: even as there be the unity of the spirit with the body.

And when thou wouldst perform thine operation during the day, arrange for the Moon to be on the ascendant, and let it be rising in one of the diurnal signs; if during the night, let it be rising in one of the nocturnal signs. And if it be rising in one of the signs of direct ascension, the work will be easier and more certain; and if it be rising in one of the signs of oblique ascension, the work will be more difficult, though the harm of these can be ameliorated by the aspects of the fortunes. Hence if it be rising in a sign of direct ascension while an infortune should occupy the same, this damages and destroys the operation, and hinders it from taking place; but if it be rising in a sign of oblique ascension while a fortune should occupy the same or behold it with a good and amicable aspect, the work will be easy to accomplish. In like manner, when the diurnal signs ascend by night and the nocturnal signs ascend by day, the beholding fortunes direct and fortify it, and the beholding infortunes destroy it. It is needful that he who intends to make an image should be altogether familiar with the signs of oblique and direct ascension; the fixed, the movable and the common; and the diurnal and the nocturnal; as well as the fortunes and infortunes, and when the Moon is safe from adverse circumstances. Let him know, too, which images are appropriate to each planet and sign. Beware as much as thou canst against performing operations that pertain to good effects when the Moon is eclipsed, or under the rays of the Sun within twelve degrees before or behind. In the same way, do thou take care against Saturn and Mars, and that it be not descending in a southerly latitude, nor in opposition thereto, when it emerges from the twelve degrees aforesaid. Take heed withal, that the Moon be not decreasing in course and slow, that is, when it proceeds less than twelve degrees in a day; for then is it assimilated to the motion of Saturn. And let it not be in the Via Combusta, which is the more to be heeded—namely, from eighteen degrees of Libra to the third degree of Scorpio—nor at the ends of the signs, which are the terms of the infortunes; nor cadent from the angle of midheaven, that is, in the ninth house. But if it should occur in any expressly necessary operations that they cannot wait for the Moon to adapt from all the abovesaid debilities, then place Jupiter and Venus on the ascendant or at midheaven; for they will rectify the debilities of the Moon.

Know that whatever we say, we speak not save to discover the secrets which are written in the books of the wise. And we pray God Almighty, in his goodness and mercy, that this book might not fall into other hands than those of wise and good men. Thou must therefore be the keeper of the aforesaid work, so that thou never revealest it to the unworthy.

BIBLIOGRAPHY

Albertus Magnus (attrib.), *Liber aggregationis*, ed. Isabelle Draelants, *Le Liber de virtutibus herbarum, lapidum et animalium* (Florence: SISMEL edizioni del Galluzzo, 2007).

Arnoldus Saxo, *De virtutibus lapidum*, ed. Valentin Rose, in *Zeitschrift für deutsches Alterthum*, 1875, 18 Bd., pp. 428–447. (N.B. A translation of this tract is in preparation by the present author).

Barrett, Francis, *The Magus* (London: Lackington, Allen & Co., 1801).

Boudet, Jean-Patrice, "Magie et illusionnisme entre Moyen Âge et Renaissance: les *Annulorum experimenta* attribués à Pietro d'Abano", in *Micrologus Library*, 50 (Florence: SISMEL edizioni del Galluzzo, 2013), pp. 247–293.

Bodin, Jean, *De la démonomanie des sorciers* (Paris: Jacques du Puys, 1581).

Damigeron, *De lapidibus*, trans. Regulus Hess, in *Celestial Gems & Sigils: De Lapidibus & Liber Sigillorum* (Renaissance Astrology, 2023), pp. 11–55.

Ferrari, Sante, *I tempi, la vita, le dottrine de Pietro d'Abano* (Genoa: 1900).

Liber Ptolomei de lapidibus preciosis et sigillis eorum, trans. Regulus Hess, in *Celestial Gems & Sigils* (Renaissance Astrology, 2023), pp. 80–104.

Peter of Abano, *Conciliator controversiarum quae inter philosophos et medicos versantur* (Venice: Juntas, 1565).

——, *De venenis eorumque remediis*, ed. Guilielmus Gratorolus

(Gratorolus, 1865?).

—— (attrib.), *Elucidation of Necromancy*, ed. and trans. Joseph H. Peterson (Lake Worth: Ibis Press, 2021).

——, *Lucidator*, ed. Graziella Federici-Vescovini, in *Pietro d'Abano, Trattati di Astronomia: "Lucidator dubitabilium astronomiae," "De motu octavae sphaerae" e altre opere* (Padua: Programma e 1+1, 1992).

Picatrix: The Latin Version of the Ghāyat Al-Ḥakīm, ed. David Pingree (London: The Warburg Institute, 1986).

Pico della Mirandola, Giovanni Francesco, *De rerum praenotione libri novem* (Strasbourg: Joannes Knoblochus, 1507).

Rankine, David, "*Annulorum Experimenta* (*Experiments of Rings*)", in *The Grimoire Encyclopedia: Volume 1* (West Yorkshire: Hadean Press, 2023), pp. 109–110.

Sadan, *Excerpta de secretis Albumasar*, ed. Graziella Federici Vescovini, "La versio latina degli *Excerpta de secretis Albumasar di Sadan*", in *Archives d'histoire doctrinale et littéraire du Moyen Age*, Vol. 65 (1998), pp. 273–330.

Theophilus, *On Divers Arts*, trans. John G. Hawthorne and Cyril Stanley Smith (New York: Dover Publications, 1979).

Thorndike, Lynn, *A History of Magic and Experimental Science, Volume II* (New York: Columbia University Press, 1923).

Skinner, Stephen, and David Rankine, *The Veritable Key of Solomon* (Singapore: Golden Hoard Press, 2021).

Zambelli, Paola, *White Magic, Black Magic in the European Renaissance* (Leiden: Brill, 2007).

INDEX

of the Rings for each Mansion from the *Annulorum Experimenta*

INDEX

of Spirits

A

B

G

H

J

L

M

Index

General

A

B

C

D

F

G

H

I

P

Q

R

S

T

V

W

www.ingramcontent.com/pod-product-compliance
Lightning Source LLC
Chambersburg PA
CBHW072156090426
42740CB00012B/2286

9781915933454